BLACK ELK

THE COMPLETE STORY

by

SAM WELLMAN

PILLARS OF THE FAITH SERIES

from

WILD CENTURIES PRESS

WILD CENTURIES PRESS
www.wildcenturies.com

Copyright © 2014 Sam Wellman

ISBN-13: 978-0-9910082-1-6

dedicated
to that glorious amateur
John G. Neihardt
who to the benefit of everyone found his 'Troy'

Unless otherwise attributed, all Scriptures taken from the
KING JAMES VERSION Holy Bible

Typefaces:
Book Antiqua
Gill Sans MT

Chapter 1

BORN LAKOTA

The Lakota named Hehaka Sapa, or 'Black Elk', was born in the moon the Cherries are Ripe in the year 'Four Crows were Killed'.[1] That seems to have been July 1863 in the words of the white-skinned people the Lakotas called wasichus. Baby Black Elk's father was also named Black Elk, and his father before him. Baby Black Elk's mother was named Leggins Down. The baby was born beside the Little Powder River, deep in the hunting grounds of the Lakota nation. Towering above the southern horizon was a colossal butte the Lakotas called Mato Tipila (or 'Den of the Bears').[2] More than one story told of Lakota children being saved from hungry bears by the prominence suddenly rising far above the ground, its vertical columns caused by bears trying to claw their way to the top.

Details of Black Elk's infancy and early childhood can be described with some certainty because Lakota life in the 1800s was very structured by custom and these customs were subsequently preserved from recollections of contemporary Lakotas. Two skilled women probably helped Leggins Down with Black Elk's birth.[3] The one who cleaned out his mouth with her finger had been chosen for her good nature because her personality would go into the baby. The second woman cleaned Black Elk with the softened inside bark of the chokecherry bush. But before she started she told the baby how hard she worked and how she tried to get along with everybody. This attitude was thought to transfer to the baby.

One of the helpers cut the umbilical cord about one hand width from the baby's navel. She inserted the cord through a prairie

---

[1] Michael F. Steltenkamp, *Black Elk: Holy Man of the Oglala* (Un. Oklahoma Press, 1993), 131, 136.
[2] Devil's Tower, a volcanic plug rising 1200 feet above the plains, is about 50 miles west-northwest of the Black Hills (Pehe Sapa).
[3] Care of babies draws mainly from Black Elk himself in Raymond J. DeMallie, editor, *The Sixth Grandfather* (Un. Nebraska Press, 1984), 379-80, 397-99, and Royal B. Hassrick, *The Sioux* (Un. Oklahoma Press, 1964), 310-316. Also, Mari Sandoz, *These were the Sioux* (NY: Hastings House, 1961) and Charles A. Eastman, *Indian Boyhood* (NY: McClure, Phillips & Co., 1902).

mushroom called a 'puffball', insuring fungus powder coated the cord. She twisted the cord and secured it to the baby with a strip of deerskin. It would drop off about four days later. The baby's cord was placed in an amulet shaped like a turtle or a lizard, both symbols of creatures hard to kill.[4] The infant would wear this amulet after beginning to walk. Such a child was spoken of 'wearing his or her navel' and this continued until the age of six or so.

After cleaning baby Black Elk one of the women oiled his skin with buffalo grease, then probably dabbed him with red paint made from earth or berries. She wrapped his bottom in skin which was packed with cattail down. The powdery down absorbed his waste and kept him dry. By the age of two months he would be in a proper 'baby bundle' of leather, usually ornately decorated.

For the first three or four days the baby sucked berry juices or broth from a leather bladder.[5] This rejection of 'first milk' was to prevent diarrhea. Then Leggins Down nursed Black Elk for two or three years. This made him strong and assured his parents there likely would be no more babies for three or so years. Black Elk as an old man remarked to twins he was a "twin himself". If literally true, the other twin must have died as an infant.[6] That might also explain another name by which he was known: Kahnigapi (Choice).[7] He did have an older brother Runs in the Center and eventually five sisters. Once Black Elk suggested he had two younger brothers.[8]

On the fourth day of his life, a 'herald' or 'crier' announced throughout the Lakota camp that the parents were hosting a feast. At this they would give gifts to many that included family members as well as the needy. Giving gifts to influential Lakotas was rare as that was considered 'buying' influence. During the feast the baby's names were announced. The 'official' one was most often the grandparent's name as it was in the case of Black Elk. Boys also had a secret name bestowed by a 'winkte'. Winktes were men who had

---

[4] Joseph Epes Brown, *Animals of the Soul* (Element Books, 1992, revised 1997), xii: To a Lakota "animals bear within them power that points to the sacred." Every animal symbolizes a sacred meaning.

[5] Hassrick (1964), 313-4. This was to avoid nursing the baby on 'first milk' or colostrum. Whether or not it was wise medically it was the custom.

[6] Black Elk may have meant symbolically a spiritual twin.

[7] DeMallie, 7-8. It was no incidental name. Many knew him only by that name. Lakotas having more than one name confused whites. And it is possible a Lakota would want to confuse them.

[8] DeMallie, 196.

souls of women. The winkte name appealed to long life because the winkte was other-worldly or sacred. However, because the name bestowed was often very bawdy it could also be used for ridicule. It was best kept secret. If Black Elk had such a name it is lost.

Like all Lakota babies, secured to a cradle board Black Elk rode back to back with his mother. She fed him her milk but did not pamper him or make too much eye contact. She discouraged his crying by pinching his nose and mouth. The camp must never be betrayed to enemies or nearby buffalo by a crying baby. Sometimes during the day Black Elk's cradle board hung on the side of the huge conical tipi of buffalo hide and poles of lodgepole pine that was the home of the Black Elks. A strap kept his shoulders and head back against the board. If the board tipped over, the cradle was deep enough to protect his head.

By being born in the heat of summer Black Elk most certainly received his first abrupt swimming lesson. At two months Lakota babies were thrown into a pond or a river and instinctively they could swim like a frog. They would be able to swim from then on. When Black Elk crawled or toddled he learned to avoid fire the hard way too. Black Elk had grandparents as well as 'second parents', who did pamper him. In doing so, his parents could and did remain stern and aloof. By the age of seven Black Elk would be discouraged from talking to his mother and even his sisters. The Lakotas had many customs that were not to be broken. All these customs had to be learned well. It was in no way a 'simple' life.

A child learned soon enough that his 'home' rarely stayed long in one place. Lakotas followed their food, primarily buffalo. And buffaloes ceaselessly moved to new supplies of grass. Moves of the Lakotas were quite structured. They could be sudden but usually they were announced a day or two in advance by the herald. Locations of tipis in the village circle were more or less rigid, thus the tipis nearest the direction of the move started out first. Property consisted of wood, leather and animals. Supplies were in leather bags. Even cooking containers were leather pouches. The tipis broke down into long lodgepoles and hides. They used the poles and hides to make travois, two poles that dragged along the ground with a hide stretched between them. Horses and dogs dragged the travois. Three or four horses were needed just to transport one average tipi. A child at an early age trudged to the next village site - not playing games but often pulling a tiny travois, The travois was loaded with as much of the family property as the child could manage. Black Elk as an infant in a cradle no doubt dangled on the side of a horse during a move, balanced by an object hanging on the other side. He might also have been on a travois or on his mother's back. Scouts led the procession, followed by the council leaders (called Wakicunsas or 'Pipe Owners'), then the general procession bounded all around by the 'akicita' (soldiers). No one was to leave the procession. Pipe Owners decided where the new camp would locate. Nearness of buffalo, water and wood was key. Other factors were protection from enemies, shelter from weather and fodder for the herd of horses. In the new location they set up camp in the same orientation as the previous one, with all tipi entrances facing east.

The tipis were ruled by the women. Men cut and stripped the heavy lodgepole pines that were as long as three men. The rest was done by women, preparing the hides and even the setting up of the tipi.[9] The base of an average tipi was about as wide as two men were tall and it was not circular but elongated so that the front was the steepest side. Such a tipi might call for 15 or more lodgepoles. The cover might require eight to ten buffalo hides. The bottom of the cover was staked down with many wooden spikes. The size of the tipi fit the family; an oversized tipi was harder to heat in cold weather. They built a fire about one-third of the way from the entrance. They controlled flaps at the top with ropes to exit smoke. They stacked wood on the south side inside the entrance. The entrance, so small it required stooping, was covered by a hide flap.

The main living area, the two-thirds west of the firepit, was covered by buffalo hides fur side up. They folded and stacked other buffalo hides, around the edges, to be used for sleeping. Some hide-covered tripods were also there for backrests. Man and wife held the place of honor at the back of the tipi. Two wives, if sisters, might share the space. They stored all supplies behind them on the west wall. Females and small children occupied the south side. Men and boys were on the north side. Guests sat just left of the man of the tipi. At night one large dog or more may have slept by the entrance. All movement within the tipi was clockwise (movement of the sun).

Over the childhood years in the tipi a Lakota absorbed the very complicated relationship of behavior between individuals, which was based on kinship.[10] Even at four or five Black Elk surely knew

---

[9] Hassrick (1964), 213-215, and many other sources.
[10] Hassrick (1964), 107-120. Also Royal B. Hassrick, "Teton Dakota Kinship System" in *American Anthropologist*, New Series, Vol. 46, (1944), 338-347, and Also James R. Walker, "Oglala Kinship Terms" in *American Anthro-*

he was supposed to call his father's brother 'father' also. And this brother's wife he called 'aunt'. His mother's sister he was to call 'mother' too. And this sister's husband he called 'uncle'. He must have noticed his father Black Elk completely shunned Plenty Eagle Feathers, the mother of Leggins Down. His father would not even look at his mother-in-law. The boy likely noted this did not offend his grandmother Plenty Eagle Feathers; in fact she acted toward Black Elk's father as if he was not even there. If his father's father had not been killed by Pawnees, the boy would have seen a similar mutual shunning between this grandfather and Leggins Down. This shunning was not hostility but a form of rigidly proper respect.

Young Black Elk surely noticed how his older brother was very cool toward their own mother. His older sisters were very cool toward their own father. Yet in some tipis he noticed the brothers in the tipi joked, even suggestively, with the wives of the other brothers. And in some tipis the sisters in the tipi joked suggestively with the husbands of the other sisters. This was an exaggerated form of familiarity, again determined by complicated kinship customs of the Lakotas. It was not at all arbitrary. Because the men in the Lakota warrior society were frequently killed in battle, their brothers took their widowed sister-in-laws as wives. It was easier when there existed between the two already a familiar relationship.

The parental tipi was formal. Such was not the case in nearby tipis of the 'second parents' or grandparents. There a boy could warm to their indulgences. And sometimes a boy could linger there and even spend the night. The father and mother of his father were dead by the time Black Elk was three. But for a long time the other grandfather, Keeps His Tipi, also called Refuses to Go, was the one Black Elk went to for advice and solace. His grandmother Plenty Eagle Feathers was still alive too and in that tipi.

At four or five a boy received his first bow and arrows. Black Elk received bows and arrows from both his father and his grandfather Keeps His Tipi.[11] Making of the bow and arrows was also dictated by custom. The length of the bow for men and boys was waist high. The Lakota bow was short and meant to be shot very quickly. A small boy's bow could be made from several kinds of wood but the preferred wood for everyone was ash. Ash was springy and resisted

---

pologist, New Series, Vol. 16, No. 1 (1914), 96-109. Walker was a physician at the Pine Ridge Agency from 1896 to 1914.

[11] DeMallie, 109, 152, 323: Black Elk related his earliest bow and arrow experiences and the Lakota boy's essential needs.

weather. The bow was strung with buffalo sinew. The best arrows were made from gooseberry or the rod-like sucker growth on cherry trees. Again, arrow size was custom. Length was equal to elbow to middle finger tip and back to the wrist. The arrow tip for a boy was blunted, later sharpened. The feathering was not from turkeys as the warriors used but usually from hawks and crows.

Black Elk as a very young boy also received a knife and a rope. Soon he began to ride a pony.[12] Boys formed stirrups with their hands and hoisted each other onto their ponies. They knew that a Lakota must mount only from the right side of the pony. But a boy had to know how to get on his pony alone. Many times a tiny boy would throw his right leg around the pony's front right leg, reach up to grasp the mane and shinny up the leg, and finally throw himself onto his pony. There was no bridle, no saddle. He gripped the mane. He formed a strong bond with his pony. After a few years the boy seemed glued to his pony, even at speed on tight turns.[13]

He knew very well he was expected to master these things and become a hunter. Black Elk felt complete with his bow and arrows, knife, rope and pony. He was only five years old. Customarily parents celebrated a boy's first bird killed. No doubt Black Elk's parents did this. But Black Elk's recollection of this early effort was overwhelmed by a vision he had while hunting birds. Already he had heard voices singing when he was four. He was probably too young to be amazed by this. But his vision at five engrossed him.

As he did so often he was practicing with his bow and arrows. He glanced up at a coming thunderstorm to the north because he heard a voice in that direction. Two men with spears erupted from a cloud. Then a nearby kingfisher alerted him: 'Look, the clouds all over are wasanica (sacred), a voice is calling you'.[14]

The two men sang.

> Behold him, a sacred voice is calling you.
> All over the sky a sacred voice is calling you.[15]

---

[12] Details from Chapter 3: 'The Indian Boy and His Pony' in Luther Standing Bear, *My Indian Boyhood* (Un. Nebraska Press, 1988, first published by Houghton Mifflin,1931), 25-44.

[13] Black Elk would discover captured horses of the wasichu, though larger and more muscular than Lakota ponies, were not as agile or as durable.

[14] The kingfisher was symbolically a messenger.

[15] DeMallie, 109.

The boy watched the approaching men for what seemed like twenty minutes. Suddenly they veered to the east and were geese.

Another time he was hunting birds in some woods. He had a wren in his sights but recalled his kingfisher vision. Birds seemed like relatives to him. How could he kill one? So he stalked a frog along a creek. His arrow killed it. It was his first kill. He was in awe by taking a life. Life was sacred. He seemed to float as he thought of the enormity of killing the frog. But he was not elated. He was overcome by the reality of what he had done.

Black Elk told no one of these moments. The Lakota boys were a rough lot. He could easily visualize the intense teasing. And his vision seemed real but unreal. Soon he had forgotten about it. His life became more and more a world of other boys.

A white soldier of the wasichus, who may well have actually seen Black Elk as a boy, wrote of the Lakotas during those days.[16]

> The slopes of the hills seemed to be covered with Indian boys, ponies, and dogs. The small boy and the big dog are two of the principal features of every Indian village... The Indian boy is far ahead of his white contemporary in healthy vigor and manly beauty. Looking at the subject as a boy would, I don't know of an existence with more happiness to the square inch...his existence is one uninterrupted gleam of sunshine. The Indian youngster knows every bird's nest for miles around, every good place for bathing, every nice pile of sand or earth to roll in. With a pony to ride and he has a pony from the time he is four years old; and a bow...

Lakota boys did indeed play at games every day. Of course shooting their arrows better and better was very important. Riding a horse well was important. Other games were skinned knuckle rough. Boys on foot would kick and trip each other and just generally wrestle and knock each other around. By six or seven they were knocking each other off their horses. It was deemed important to tease and needle constantly. A boy must not be soft. Nor should he get too high an opinion of himself. The games became increasingly painful. One game was to flip mud from the end of a stick. It sounded weak but in fact the mud stung the skin like a hornet. Any of these games could erupt into a real knock-down, bruising fight.

---

[16] John G. Bourke, *On the Border with Crook* (Un. Nebraska Press, 1971, first published, 1891), 410.

They pinched, they pulled and plucked hair. They burned each other in a game called "setting fire to your skin". They would put pith from a weed on their arm and light it. The weak boys had to brush the fire off. The bravest let it burn all the way down. That was not the end to the ways they tortured each other. The scariest was "fox choking". A boy was choked into unconsciousness with a strip of fox hide. During the choking and when he woke up he twitched and jerked convulsively. This delighted the other boys. The object was for the victim never to show pain. They knew by then their destiny was to be warriors. Someday they would fight warriors of another language and show them Lakotas were oblivious to pain. They had to be willing to kill and also to be killed.

The Lakota boys also soon understood they were to be more than warriors, They were to be nomadic warriors who lived off the nomadic buffalo. The massive grazers furnished far more than fresh meat and jerky. They gave every particle of their bodies for some Lakota need, right down to the ribs bound together to make sleds for games in the snow. Lakotas over the eons had learned to use parts of the buffalo for glue, dyes, soap, rope, dice, fuel, hide, clothing, tipi covers, powder horns, tanning agents, pouches, shields, thongs, thread and dozens of other needs. The boys also learned that great trackers and hunters of buffalo were almost as praised and touted as great warriors.

Black Elk soon knew the Lakotas of his village moved around in an area cut by four major south-to-north rivers that flowed north into the Yellowstone River. From west to east the four rivers were the Bighorn, the Rosebud, the Tongue and the Powder. East of these areas was one renegade river - the Belle Fourche - that flowed east. All of this grassland plain was just west of their sacred mountains they called the Pehe Sapa ('Black Hills').

But Black Elk seemed destined to be more than a warrior or hunter. His father Black Elk and several of his father's brothers were healers, as was their father who was also called Black Elk. They were neither strictly wicasa wakan (holy men) with mystical powers nor strictly pejuta wicasa (medicine men) who used medicines and herbs to heal. They were wapiyapi[17] (healers) who used everything at their disposal including medicine and mystical power. Black Elk by the age of five had to know this. For at five, he had already experienced his first vision, although he told no one.

---

[17] DeMallie, 102.

Chapter 2

THE WORLD OF THE LAKOTA

By 1870 young Black Elk had some grasp of a greater world than his wandering village. The Black Elk family belonged to a group of Lakotas headed by chief Big Road. There were about a dozen bands (tiospayes) of Lakotas like Big Road's group. The entire assembly of groups was a 'council fire' (ospaye) called Oglala. [18] Each of the dozen or so tiospayes had several hundred Oglalas. Black Elk would learn these bands grew and evaporated according to the strength of their warriors. One band strong today could disappear on some tomorrow or may not have existed in the long gone days.[19]

Big Road's band intermingled mostly with other Oglala groups headed by Red Cloud, Little Hawk and Crazy Horse. These four were the northern groups of Oglalas. Black Elk's grandfather was the brother of the grandfather of the two Oglala Lakota half-brothers Crazy Horse and Little Hawk. It was some time before young Black Elk knew what the much older Crazy Horse meant to the Lakotas. Besides the ospaye of Oglala Lakotas there were six other ospayes or 'council fires' of Lakotas. Especially numerous and strong - like the Oglalas - were the ospayes called Minneconjous, Hunkpapas and Brules,. Less numerous were the ospayes of Black Feet, Sans Arcs and Two Kettles. All Lakotas were kin to each other.

> The Lakota are allied against all others of mankind, though they may war among themselves. They are oyate ikce (native people), and are ankantu (superior), while all others of mankind are oyate unma (other-people), who are ihukuya (considered -inferior). This is the relation of the Lakota to all others of mankind...[20]

---

[18] George Hyde, *Red Cloud's Folk* (Un. Oklahoma Press, 1937, revised 1957 and 1975), 8-9, suggested Oglala, translated 'scattered', comes from the time they left Minnesota woodlands to scatter west across the prairies.

[19] Hyde, *Red Cloud's Folk*, 308-315, discusses in a non-rigorous way the transient nature of tiospayes.

[20] James R. Walker, 'Oglala Kinship Terms' (1914), 96-109.

It was familiar tribal doxology of 'we the chosen ones' against the less gifted others. In fact, relationships of the Lakotas to oyate unma (others) had evolved over the decades. Lakotas during Black Elk's boyhood were especially friendly with the Arapahoes and the Cheyennes (or Shyela). On the other hand, Lakotas were especially bitter enemies to the Crows to the north, to the Shoshones to the west and to the Pawnees to the south.

In the matter of marriage, it was best that the Oglala man not take a woman from his own camp. If at all possible she should come from another of the dozen or so bands of Oglalas. Best of all was that she come from one of the other six ospayes or 'council fires'. For example, the mother of the Oglala Crazy Horse was from the Minneconjou ospaye; his later two stepmothers were the sisters of Spotted Tail, a chief of the Brule ospaye. That Crazy Horse's two stepmothers were sisters also shows that if a Lakota marries a woman with younger sisters he has first claim on them and if he takes a sister as wife she can live in the same tipi. If he takes another woman as wife she must establish her own tipi. A man may also take a captive woman as wife but she must establish her own tipi and conform to customs of the Lakota. The Lakota wife owned the tipi and everything in it except the man's clothing and goods. The children were hers unless she was a captive. Children belonged first to their mother, then to their father, then to their father's camp.

The Lakota man was nevertheless the head of the family, and virtually owned his wife. After all, he had paid for her - perhaps twelve buffalo robes or a certain number of horses. He could beat her if he wished but he could not cripple her or kill her. If he did, her immediate family (wico-we) could maim him, even kill him. On the other hand he could abandon a wife at his pleasure, or even present her to another man as a gift, either temporary or permanent. To offer a wife temporarily was the greatest courtesy that could be shown.[21] To refuse such courtesy was a grave insult. The wife however could not abandon the man without his consent. If she did it anyway, she lost all her rights to the tipi and the children. She became a lone-woman (wino-wanzica). And the man was free to maim her, often by cutting off her nose or one of her ears. If however this abandonment was by a childless woman who left to become the woman of a more powerful warrior she had that warrior's protection.

---

[21] Walker, 'Oglala Kinship Terms' (1914), 100.

BLACK ELK

At Black Elk's birth the nearest bluecoat soldiers of the wasichus (white people) were at Fort Laramie, a stronghold in the distant south separated by several days of riding. It was not however an idyllic time for Lakotas. Other wasichus - trappers and prospectors - seemed very numerous and they might be found anywhere poking around. These the Lakotas usually killed if the intruders were unknown. White women or children however might be taken into the band.[22] The whites had discovered the yellow metal they loved to the northwest in the land of the Bannacks. Now whites streamed right through the Powder River country of the Lakotas to look hungrily for the yellow metal.

Rumors said the whites were fighting and killing each other far to the east. Wise Lakota elders knew when that 'Civil War' ended many more bluecoated soldiers would probably be coming to Lakota lands. The procedure of the whites was already known. They found good trails, usually of course trails blazed by native people, then built forts along those trails. Bluecoated soldiers then guarded the trails. One great trail along the North Platte River was the Oregon Trail and sometimes wagons full of whites traveled west on the trail twenty abreast. Soon the trail north to the yellow metal in the land of the Bannacks might be like that. It was called the Bozeman Road. It was particularly irksome because it snaked right through the Powder River country of the Lakotas. The leader of one band of the Oglalas, Red Cloud, was known to cooperate with the whites. But even he was angry with Bozeman Road, murderously angry. He was as determined as other Lakotas to close it down.

In July 1865 a great army of Lakotas - Oglalas, Brules and Minneconjous - and their friends the Cheyennes went right to the source, to the North Platte River bridge where the Bozeman Road left the Oregon Trail and headed north. War leaders included many chiefs of later legend: Crazy Horse, Red Cloud and Young Man Afraid of his Horses of the Lakotas plus Roman Nose and Dull Knife of the Cheyennes. This army had perhaps 3000 warriors. There were no more than 150 bluecoats guarding the bridge. It was wonderful weather to fight. Lakotas liked to strip down to nothing

---

[22] An example is Fanny Kelly, *Narrative of my captivity among the Sioux Indians* (Cincinnati: Wilstach, Baldwin & Co., 1871). She was captured July 1864 on the Oregon Trail (in present-day Wyoming) by a large party of Oglalas led by chief Ottowa (or Silver Horn). All white men with Fanny either escaped or were killed. Whites bartered her release five months later.

more than their breech cloth or even naked except a waist band. They fastened a rope from their horse to the waist band, so if they fell off the horse it could not bolt away. They yelled "Hoka hey!" for 'Onward!' or 'Hurry!' Some yelled 'It's a good day to die!'

The problem the Lakotas had with a sustained attack was that they had few guns and even less ammunition.[23] Bows and arrows were not effective against an entrenched enemy with rifles. The enemy had to be lured into the open or into a trap. Neither lure happened at the North Platte River bridge. Lakotas and Cheyennes were not foolish in battle. They did not charge recklessly into firing guns. Some like Crazy Horse were defiant and seemed bullet-proof but they were exceptions. As a result of the bluecoats remaining hunkered down, the immense force of Lakotas and Cheyennes killed only 29 of them. Within a few days the 3000 attackers ran low on food and drifted back to their distant villages.

By 1866 the bluecoats had built three forts on the Bozeman Road. Fort Smith, Fort Kearny and Fort Reno were both no more than two days of hard riding from the Little Powder River, so bluecoated soldiers were now much closer to the Big Road Band than before. At this time Crazy Horse was a chief of lesser stature than Red Cloud but he was a master at warfare. Both he and Red Cloud and other Oglalas including Big Road harassed the bluecoats continually in groups of several dozen warriors. They were joined by the Lakota groups of Brules and Minneconjous. Even two friendly tribes participated: Cheyennes and Arapahoes. In December 1866 north of Fort Kearny, ten warriors decoyed a detachment of 79 bluecoats and two civilians into a canyon near the Tongue River.[24] It was a trap and hundreds of Lakotas, Cheyennes and Arapahoes rained bullets and arrows from every direction. They killed all 81 whites. Black Elk's own father was in the fight and suffered a severe broken leg. The Lakotas, Cheyennes and Arapahoes may have lost as few as 13 on the battlefield. Right after the fight however the area was struck by a blizzard, which resulted in many of the wounded dying. The

---

[23] Stanley Vestal, *Sitting Bull: Champion of the Sioux* (Houghton Mifflin, 1932), 183, asserted that Crazy Horse had one of the most warlike of all the bands and the best armed. Even at that, probably only one-half of his 300 or so warriors had guns.

[24] Mari Sandoz, *Crazy Horse: the strange man of the Oglalas* (NY: Alfred E. Knopf, 1942) created the fiction that Crazy Horse was one of the decoys, perhaps their leader. Like John Neihardt she did not allow a fact to get in the way of a good story.

Lakotas called this lopsided fight the Battle of the Hundred Slain. The wasichus called it the Fetterman Massacre, after the bluecoat officer foolish enough to fall into the trap.

Whites claimed later that the bluecoats and two civilians were horribly mutilated. One civilian had more than 100 arrows in him. Others were cut up in grisly ways. The only one spared mutilation was a 16-year-old bugler who had fought valiantly to the end with no weapon but his battered bugle. Lakotas greatly respected courage in battle. But some said the more mutilated a body was the more that enemy had been respected.[25] The white people were so stunned by this gruesome defeat and continuing skirmishes like the 'Wagon Box Fight' they closed the three forts on the Bozeman Road. Lakotas like Crazy Horse however were not satisfied with this victory, harboring a deep distrust for the whites.

Black Elk was probably aware at the time in 1869 or later that the Hunkpapas captured a mail carrier far to the north near the Milk River in the moon of Frost in the Tipi (January). Instead of killing him Sitting Bull took a liking to him. Sitting Bull named this Frank Grouard the 'Grabber' because Grouard was a huge man totally garbed in buffalo fur and Grouard looked like a grasping bear fighting off his attackers with just his hands. To all appearances Grouard was a Lakota, although he claimed to be an islander from a great ocean far beyond the western horizon. But in no time at all Grabber was speaking Lakota like he was born to it. No Lakota believed that Grabber was not half or full Lakota. Grabber was soon put to the test with the Lakota tortures designed to test courage. He later claimed they cut 480 pea-sized pieces of flesh out of *each* arm.[26] That was followed by hair-plucking and the burning of pith on his arms. Grouard endured the excruciating pain by remaining stoic and most Lakotas liked the huge man.[27]

Just how much they liked him was proven later when he had a falling out with Sitting Bull. He had been living in the tipi of Sitting

---

[25] Vestal, *Sitting Bull*, 174, insists the opposite was true. The Lakota most mutilated the bravest enemy, so he would be completely destroyed.

[26] Grouard, as related in Joe de Barthe, *Life and Adventures of Frank Grouard* (St. Joseph, MO: Combe Printing Co., 1894), 120.

[27] Nettie Goings, who claimed to be Grouard's half-sister, said he was the son of a Creole cook and a Lakota woman far to the north on the Missouri River. Although the Lakotas themselves and many bluecoats liked Grouard, some later scholars of the Crazy Horse story loathe him, blaming him for many deceits.

Bull's sister but he lied to the chief about how he had stolen three horses that he gave Sitting Bull's family as gifts. Sitting Bull found out it was a lie and was enraged. Grouard had been in Sitting Bull's camp for three years but had to leave it to join the camp of Oglalas under Crazy Horse. It seemed even the ever suspicious Crazy Horse liked Grouard. Certainly Grouard bore pain like a warrior. But he was also a crack shot and good provider of buffalo. He was an outstanding tracker too. He would emerge later as a significant player in the fate of all the Lakotas.

The Lakotas did not fight only the bluecoats. They fought all enemies - 'tokoyapi' - especially those intruding on their hunting grounds. Although the Cheyennes and Arapahoes were friendlies, the Crows, Shoshones and Pawnees definitely were not. Killing 'tokoyapi' was so important that many engagements with them were recorded as the great event of the year on the 'winter count', represented by graphic pictures inscribed on a buffalo hide. The winter count of Brule Lakota Battiste Good, also called Brown Hat, is often cited because it is known to be accurate. For an example of killing 'tokoyapi', the 1870-1871 pictograph from his winter count shows symbols indicating a fight at a fort.[28] At the mouth of the Musselshell River on the Upper Missouri River was a trading post for the Crows. Hunkpapa Lakotas attacked the Crows there, killing 29 Crows while losing 14 of their own.

It is strange that an engagement with the Flatheads[29] in 1871 is not the great event in the winter count. But Black Elk's much later account of the incident revealed the Lakotas considered them unworthy, a pitiful enemy. The event "Came-and-killed-High-Back-Bone" was more significant for that year. The Minneconjou chief, also called Hump, was a great older friend of Crazy Horse. Shoshones killed him with a rifle from long range, somewhat ironic because Hump was armed with a pistol he apparently took great pride in.

Nevertheless the triumph over the Flatheads in 1871 was much discussed among Lakotas when Black Elk was a boy of seven. The Flatheads usually hunted considerably west of the Lakota hunting grounds. The Lakotas however had expanded their territory to the west, taking lands from the Crows. The Lakotas had a large camp at

---

[28] Garrick Mallery, *Picture-Writing of the American Indians* (Smithsonian Institution, Bureau of American Ethnology Annual Report 10, 1893), 287, figure 255. Good was born in 1821 or 1822.

[29] the 'Salish', which also included the Kootenai and Pend d'Oreilles.

the mouth of the Rosebud where it joined the Yellowstone.[30] Most were Hunkpapas but Oglalas, Minneconjous and Sans Arcs were there too.

Scouts reported many Flatheads on the Musselshell River. They found a camp of about 100 tipis. The main body of Lakotas remained about two miles from the Flathead camp while a small band of Lakota crept up to the camp and then very openly stole some Flathead horses and fled back toward the main group. Dozens of Flatheads swarmed after them into the trap. Then the main group of Lakota sprang from their ambush. They slaughtered the greatly outnumbered Flatheads. The Lakotas claimed 66 dead Flatheads.[31] A number of Lakotas were wounded, including Sitting Bull. Two Lakotas had been killed outright and three wounded died later.

This battle was typical for the 1860s and early 1870s: The Hunkpapas generally ranged north of the Black Hills and were in constant conflicts with other Native Americans, especially the Crows. The Oglalas ranged just west of the Black Hills and skirmished frequently with the bluecoats. But as the Frank Grouard story illustrates, serious strife took place within the Lakota tipis too. In the summer of 1870 Crazy Horse had taken Black Buffalo Woman from the warrior No Water. The maddened No Water burst into the tipi of Crazy Horse and shot him in the face. The bullet entered his face beside his nose, went through the palate and emerged from his neck. Miraculously Crazy Horse lived, powder burns permanently marring his left cheek along with a prominent white scar that at times contorted his mouth into a grimace.[32]

To make Crazy Horse even more miserable that summer of 1870 was the news that his half-brother Little Hawk had been killed in the south not by their traditional enemies but by renegade white

---

[30] Vestal, *Sitting Bull*, 122-126, relates the Flathead encounter. Vestal got much of his information from White Bull, who was the nephew of Sitting bull. White Bull never seemed to miss an opportunity to pump up the achievements of Sitting Bull or himself and to disparage the achievements of Crazy Horse. In spite of that, the general account is probably reliable.

[31] Sixty six were claimed by Black Elk in DeMallie, 337. White Bull claimed thirty.

[32] Bourke, 415, described him in 1877 as "quite young, not over thirty years old, five feet eight inches high, lithe and sinewy, with a scar in the face. The expression of his countenance was one of quiet dignity, hut morose, dogged, tenacious, and melancholy. He behaved with stolidity, like a man who realized he had to give in to Fate, but would do so as sullenly as possible."

men.³³ The other Oglalas had used caution and fled against gunfire but typical of Little Hawk he was reckless in battle, even more reckless than Crazy Horse. He charged right in against the guns. He had not possessed the invincibility that Crazy Horse seemed to have.³⁴ Of course even seven-year-old Black Elk, as an Oglala and relative of Little Hawk and Crazy Horse, knew of these happenings.

To infuriate Crazy Horse and other Lakotas was the fact that that the Treaty supposedly closing the Bozeman Road proved a sham. Perhaps the army had withdrawn open support of the road but less visibly the army was exploring both the Black Hills area and the Yellowstone River area for the white and yellow metals they so craved. The Lakotas also heard whites were surveying so they could build a railroad east to west, right through their hunting grounds.³⁵ Whites told a half truth about their railroads. They said they were to get people through Lakota country to the west coast. But the whole truth was that many people came on the railroad to stay in the Lakota country. This the Lakotas had already learned with the intrusion of the Union Pacific Railroad along the North Platte River. Settlers were claiming land all along the periphery of the railroad.

Getting wind of this survey party for construction of a northern railroad in early August 1873 along the Yellowstone River were nearby Hunkpapas, Oglalas, Minneconjous and Cheyennes. The Hunkpapas included Gall, Rain in the Face and even Frank Grouard. The Oglalas were led by none other than Crazy Horse. A few miles west of where the Tongue flowed into Yellowstone River the intruders were discovered by the Lakotas and Cheyennes. The surveyors were guarded by 100 or so bluecoats. The bluecoats were commanded by a vain, flashy soldier named George Custer.

The Lakotas tried to decoy the bluecoats toward an ambush. They sprang the trap but Custer managed to retreat into a dry river

---

³³ There is much confusion over the name 'Little Hawk'. Crazy Horse's father Worm had a half-brother also named 'Little Hawk'. He was very influential with Crazy Horse and to make the confusion worse, although Little Hawk was the 'uncle' of Crazy Horse he was only four or five years older than Crazy Horse.

³⁴ This belief was widespread among friends and foes. Edward S. Curtis, *The North American Indian*, V. 3 (Cambridge: University Press, 1908), 21: General Crook claimed that in the Battle of the Rosebud in 1876 he had 20 easy rifle shots at Crazy Horse, who always came very close to the enemy. Every shot missed.

³⁵ Northern Pacific Railroad.

channel, then dismount with every eighth trooper holding the horses. The other troopers, well-armed with repeating rifles, set up a skirmish line behind the river bank. The Lakotas tried to flank the bluecoats but failed. They set a grass fire thinking they might attack the bluecoats through the smoke. That also failed. The skirmish lasted three hours in intense heat. The cavalry lost 11 men. The Lakotas and Cheyennes lost about five warriors.[36]

That very summer of 1873 Lakotas were also far to the southeast, so far that they were south of the Platte River. In July 700 Pawnees, half of whom were women and children, set out for their summer buffalo hunt for meat and leather. Most Pawnee men had only bows and arrows or old fashioned muzzle loading rifles. They had with them 800 extra ponies to pack the meat and hides. Several whites tried to warn the Pawnees that many Oglalas and Brules were also hunting in the area. Pawnee leader Sky Chief said the whites were just lying so the whites would get to the buffalo instead of them.

The attack on the Pawnees was instigated by the so-called Cut-Off band of Oglalas under Little Wound. It did not bode well that one of the Oglala chiefs was called Pawnee Killer. The Oglalas invited a very large force of Brules under Spotted Tail to join them. On August 5, over 1000 Lakota warriors engaged the Pawnees and virtually forced them to descend into a canyon that led down toward the Republican River. The Lakotas fired down into the Pawnees from both sides of the canyon. According to the Pawnee agent John Williamson, who was there that day, the Lakotas lost about 50 warriors while killing 156 Pawnees, including Sky Chief.[37]

Black Elk was nine years old in that Pawnee-killing summer of 1873. He was at the time in the Rosebud country.[38] In fact that was the summer when young Black Elk had his great vision.

---

[36] Because Rain in the Face supposedly bragged about killing the cavalry's veterinarian, over a year later George Custer's brother Tom arrested him and hassled him. A story goes that Rain in the Face vowed to one day cut out the heart of Tom Custer and eat it. Rain in the Face may have done just that at the Battle of the Little Bighorn.

[37] John Williamson, 'Last buffalo hunt of the Pawnees,' in Samuel Clay Bassett, *History of Buffalo Count, Nebraska, and Its People* (Chicago: S.J. Clarke Publishing, 1916), 383-388. Some scholars place the number of dead Pawnees at 69 and dead Lakotas at just six.

[38] Black Elk's narrative in DeMallie (1984), 111, hints that the Big Road band may have participated in the slaughter of the Pawnees but that is unlikely.

Chapter 3

BLACK ELK'S GREAT VISION OF 1873

Standing Bear was about 13 years old in June 1873. The Oglalas under Big Road were camped at the headwaters of the Greasy Grass (Little Bighorn) River. Standing Bear heard Black Elk, just nine years old, was dying. No one else was sick at all. Boys had been out riding, stopped to water their ponies and Black Elk just fell to the ground. When Standing Bear visited the tipi, he saw Black Elk unconscious and barely breathing.[39]

It would be several years before Black Elk would reveal what happened to him. The day before his collapse he was eating with Man Hip in his tipi when he heard a voice call, "It is time now. They are calling you." He realized at the time the spirits were calling him. His thighs were aching when he left Man Hip. Next morning when he was out with the boys he dropped to the ground. By the time the boys had taken him to his tipi his legs and arms were swollen.

As he lay unconscious in the tipi his vision began.[40]

Nearly sixty years later he would recall this vision as follows.

Two men came down out of the clouds. They were the same two men who had been in his vision four years earlier. They beckoned him, "Hurry up, your grandfather is calling you."

Black Elk, riding a small cloud, followed them.

A bay horse appeared and spoke to him. "Behold me. My life history you shall see. Furthermore, behold them, those where the sun goes down, their lives' history you shall see."

To the west were 12 black horses, each with a necklace of buffalo hoofs. Above them flew birds, probably swallows symbolic of thunder beings because all around them was thunder and lightning.

Then to the north Black Elk saw 12 white horses with necklaces of elk teeth that meant long life. Flying over them were white geese.

To the east were 12 sorrel horses, but with horns. Eagles were soaring above them.

---

[39] Standing Bear's recollection is from DeMallie (1984), 143.
[40] Quotes are from Black Elk's narration of his 1873 vision detailed in DeMallie (1984), 111-142. DeMallie's description of over 12,000 words is by necessity shortened, hopefully without omitting any key elements.

To the south were 12 buckskin horses, also with horns. Over them were soaring Hawks.

The bay horse told Black Elk his grandfathers were having a council and would see him. He should be brave. The four groups of 12 horses lined up. It seemed all around Black Elk there were horses of every color. The bay would neigh to them and they would neigh back. The bay led Black Elk, followed by the four groups of 12 horses. The bay horse said to Black Elk, "Behold, your horses are dancing." Now the sky was swirling with other horses, it seemed millions, but they changed into buffalo and other animals that disappeared into the four directions.

Inside a rainbow door in a rainbowed gate were the six grandfathers. On either side of Black Elk were the first two men of his vision. The groups of 12 horses returned to their original four directions. One of the grandfathers asked him to enter and the four groups of horses neighed encouragement.

The western grandfather told Black Elk that he would share his willpower, so Black Elk will have power to use on earth. He gave Black Elk a bow and arrow. "Depend on this, for you shall go against our enemies and you shall be a great warrior." He said further, "You shall be very powerful on earth in medicines and all powers. He is your spirit and you are his body and his name is Eagle Wing Stretches." He then gave Black Elk a wooden cup of water. "Behold, take this, and with this you shall be great."[41]

That grandfather ran west where he turned into a black horse that began to shrivel and die. The grandfather from the north urged a holy herb on Black Elk, who brandished it toward the dying black horse. The horse immediately fattened up and recovered. The northern grandfather told Black Elk he would create a nation.[42]

Then the grandfather from the north ran toward the north and changed into a white goose.[43] Black Elk now saw thunder in the west and white geese in the north.

The first grandfather sang:

> They are appearing, may you behold.
> They are appearing, may you behold.
> The thunder nation is appearing, may you behold.

---

[41] Later to Black Elk that meant he could cure all sickness with that water.
[42] To Black Elk later that would mean he was going to cure lots of sickness.
[43] To Black Elk that later meant he would make everybody cry as geese do when they fly north in the spring because hardship is over.

The second grandfather sang:

> They are appearing, may you behold.
> They are appearing, may you behold
> The white geese nation is appearing, may you behold.

The third grandfather, of the south, pointed to the morning star, also called the daybreak star. Below the star were two men flying. He said they would give Black Elk power. The third grandfather also held a peace pipe, with a spotted eagle on the handle. He said, "With this whatever is sick on this earth you shall make well."

Then the third grandfather pointed at a man solid red in color. The red man lay down and changed into a buffalo, then ran to the east and in this direction all the horses turned into buffalo.

Then the fourth grandfather, of the east, told Black Elk he now had the power of all four quarters. At that, Black Elk saw that in each direction there now stood a chief.[44] The fourth grandfather gave Black Elk a branch that was budding and about to flower. The grandfather said, "With this, brace yourself as with a cane and that way your nation will brace itself as with a cane and with this cane you shall make a nation."

Grandfather of the east told Black Elk there was a sacred road that ran north and south. That road was red and from it everything is good. On the other hand, there was a black road that ran west and east. It was a road of thunder beings, a destructive road.

With that, the grandfather of the east rolled on the ground, became a horse, then became an elk, before running south to the buckskins where they all turned into elks.

The fifth grandfather, who represented Wakan Tanka or the Great Spirit above, said, "Behold me, my power you shall see." He spread his arms and turned into a spotted eagle. "The sky things shall be like relatives. Your grandfathers shall attack an enemy and be unable to destroy him, but with my power you will be able to destroy the enemy."

The sixth grandfather, who was the spirit below on earth, was a very old man with white hair. He said: "Boy, you want my power on earth, so you shall know me. You shall have my power in going back to the earth. Your nation on earth shall have great difficulties. There you shall go. Behold me as I depart."

---

[44] To Black Elk later that meant he would have become the most powerful medicine man of all time if the Lakotas had not changed after submitting to the white men.

BLACK ELK

Black Elk watched the sixth grandfather, who had a spear in his hand. The very old man got younger and younger until he was a little boy nine years old. Black Elk knew he was looking at himself.

Black Elk held a wooden cup of water with which he was to save mankind with his medicine. He also had a bow and arrow, with which he was going to destroy the enemy. He was now mounted on the bay horse. Behind him were all the blacks, whites, sorrels, buckskins. They all faced north.

The north had given him the holy herb with the power to save horses.

The east had given him the peace pipe to also cure the sick on this earth.

The east had also given Black Elk the power of the black sacred road, a road of the thunder beings that made beings all over the universe fear him.

Now 12 riders were him, all righthanded but one. They called Black Elk by the name of Eagle That Stretches Its Wing. The riders and horses were decorated with hail, the symbol of the thunder beings. As they rode the black sacred road eastward from the highest peak in the west Black Elk saw every being on earth was trembling with fear. As they neared the forks of the Missouri River Black Elk saw a man standing in flames. Dead creatures were all around him. He was the enemy.

Black Elk and his riders sang a song that represented all four directions:

> I, myself, have sent them a-fleeing
> Because I wore the feather of an eagle.
> I, myself, sent them a-fleeing.

> I, myself, have sent them a-fleeing
> For I wore the relic of the wind.
> I, myself, have sent them a-fleeing

Then the Thunder-beings sang:

> I, myself, send them a-fleeing
> For I wore the relic of the hail.
> I, myself, send them a-fleeing

Then the ones on the west sang:

> I, myself, send them a-fleeing
> I, myself, send them a-fleeing

The 12 riders from the west attacked this man but could not destroy him. Then riders from the north failed. Then the east, then the south. They all failed to destroy him. Black Elk saw a blue man rise splashing from water and charge him. Black Elk's bow and arrow changed into a spear. With the spear and the cup of water Black Elk charged the blue man. He lanced the blue man through the heart. He withdrew the spear and the blue man turned into a turtle. All that had been dead came alive. All were cheering Black Elk.[45]

Next, Black Elk found himself on earth along the Missouri River. There he came upon a village in a circle. On the south side of the village the southern grandfather told him that the village was Black Elk's nation and gave him the stick sprouting branches. He was to give his nation the sprouting stick along with the peace pipe. They were to walk the sacred red road to the north.

On the east side of the village was a tipi off by itself. Around it people were dying. One man, who was turning gray, had flames coming from his mouth. The wind was blowing south to north. As Black Elk passed the tipi all the people recovered. The southern grandfather told him that was the way he would save people.[46]

Then Black Elk was taken to the center of the village, where the southern grandfather told him to give his nation the peace pipe and sprouting stick. His nation was to have them for peace and health. The southern grandfather said that his nation should walk the sacred red road from south to north. The northern grandfather then added that he had given Black Elk the holy herb and the wind. Black Elk was to give them to his nation. This village should now break camp and walk the road.[47]

The people wanted to pray to the spirits. One grandfather called to the people, "Behold your grandfathers are walking with you." They broke camp and riders carried the gifts from the grandfathers.

The rider on the black horse carried the herb. The white horse rider had the sacred wind. The sorrel rider held the sacred pipe. The buckskin rider had the sprouting branch. All of the people of the village were going along. Four other riders, one from each direction, came up and gave Black Elk a sacred hoop, with which the nation was to prosper.

The western grandfather held in his left hand the hoop and in his right hand the bow and arrow. "With this nation and with this

---

[45] Black Elk thought later this meant he was going to kill an enemy in battle.
[46] To Black Elk later that meant he was to be a wakan wicasa or 'holy man'.
[47] Black Elk thought that meant his nation was to prosper.

bow and arrow you shall conquer your worst enemy on earth."[48] The western grandfather also held the wooden cup of water and said, "This will tame your wildest enemies." But water also had the power to heal. The grandfathers talked much of the various powers given Black Elk.

Black Elk's nation chose four chiefs and four advisors. The people of his nation walked north on the sacred red road in formation:

> First, the four spirit horsemen.
> Second, the four chiefs.
> Third, the four advisors.
> Fourth, old men with canes.
> Fifth, old women with canes.
> Last, Black Elk himself at the rear.

The southern grandfather sang a song to the future nation:

> A voice I am sending as I walk.
> A voice I am sending as I walk.
> A sacred hoop I wore.
> Thus, a voice I send as I walk.
> Thus, a voice I send as I walk.

The first child he called was named Spotted Deer Woman, calling unborn children. Next he called was Young Buffalo Woman. He went through four generations. One of the old men, noted the sacred hoop and said, "Behold a good nation, a sacred nation, again they will walk toward good land, the land of plenty, and there will be no suffering."[49]

The first future generation sang.

> May you behold this I have asked to be made over.
> May you behold this I have asked to be made over.
> A good nation I have asked to be made over.
> May you behold this I have asked to be made over.
> May you behold this I have asked to be made over.
> A sacred nation I have asked to be made over.
> May you behold this I have asked to be made over.
> May you behold this I have asked to be made over.

---

[48] He said it in such a way it meant Black Elk would be a chief of that nation.
[49] Black Elk thought he had been given the power to raise a nation.

They were asking to be strengthened spiritually, even made over spiritually.

The people sang into the second generation too. But they stopped there. Though those two generations were fated to be good Black Elk later felt something bad was in the future for the third generation. The next generation seemed even more foreboding.[50]

Further into vision, regarding the fourth generation, the southern grandfather said, "Look upon your nation." The people were all desperately poor. Many children were pale and sick. Black Elk's nation appeared dying.[51] To soften the effect the vision again began to tout the gifts, or powers, given to Black elk.

Now on the north side of his village (nation), Black Elk saw a man painted red and holding a spear. The red man walked into the center of the hoop and rolled on the ground. He became a buffalo. It rolled and became the holy herb. The herb plant grew and bloomed so that Black Elk could see what it really looked like. The wind in the form of a spirit blew and all things lived again and flourished.

A grandfather said, "You have seen the powers of the north in the forms of man, buffalo, herb and wind. The people will follow the man's steps. They will live like the buffalo. With the herb they will have knowledge. They will be relatives to the wind."[52]

Again, with the village as the backdrop the grandfathers enumerated the gifts: the herb, the sacred pipe, the hoop, the flowering stick, the cup of water and the bow and arrow. Then they told Black Elk they had shown him everything there was to do on earth and that he was now to do it himself.

One the grandfathers sang this so Black Elk could sing it:

> A good nation I will make over.
> The nation above has said this to me.
> They have given me the power to make over this nation.

The people in his nation shouted, "Eagle Wing Stretches, thank you!" They started on the good road, the red road, and Black Elk was forced to give all his gifts to the people, with the exception of

---

[50] Years later Black Elk interpreted the third and fourth generations as enduring the horrors of World War I and World War II.

[51] The fourth generation seemed so far in the future to nine-year-old Black Elk that it did not make the impression that it would make years later.

[52] Black Elk would later transform this to the people being healthy like the man, getting meat from the buffalo, getting knowledge of diseases from the herb. They would get endurance from the north wind.

the bow and arrow. The people accepted what Black Elk gave them. The horses became fat, so the people began to break camp.

Black Elk went ahead on the good road with the riders. Black Elk saw a flame coming up from the earth. They went to it, thunder and lightning all around. Black Elk heard his people on the good road ask, "Who killed that enemy?" Someone answered that Eagle Wing Stretches has done it and they all cheered. Black Elk had killed it within the flames. He looked at it and realized it was a dog. One side of the dog was white and the other side was black.[53]

The western grandfather said they were going to show Black Elk a 'flipping'. They showed him a black horse, so emaciated it was skin and bones. Then the grandfather gave Black Elk an herb and urged him on. Black Elk made the' circle over the horse. The horse rolled, changing into a powerful shiny black stallion. He had dapples and seemed of thunder and lightning. He faced west and neighed. From the west came a million horses. The black stallion neighed to the north. Again, millions of horses came toward them. The black stallion did the same thing to the east and west.

The western grandfather said, "These are your horses. Your horses shall dance for you." The grandfather sang a song.[54]

> My horses prancing they are coming from all over the universe.
> My horses neighing they are coming, prancing they are coming.
> All over the universe my horses are coming.

The dappled black stallion sang this song:

> They will dance, may you behold them.
> They will dance, may you behold them.
> They will dance, may you behold them.
> They will dance, may you behold them.
> A horse nation will dance, may you behold them.
> A horse nation will dance, may you behold them.
> A horse nation will dance, may you behold them.
> A horse nation will dance, may you behold them.

The voice of the dappled black stallion boomed all over the universe. It was so delightful no one could resist dancing. Deer and the

---

[53] Later Black Elk thought the two colors meant the dog can be a friend or can be an enemy.
[54] A song that Black Elk later called the 'horse dance'.

buffalo were leaping and running. Even leaves on trees danced. Creeks were singing. Black Elk had such power every living creature was happy.

The western grandfather said, "This day is yours. Now we will take you to the center of the earth."

This was a high mountain where Black Elk could see all over the earth. All sixteen riders of the four directions were with him. They faced east and two men with wings rushed from the east. They came to Black Elk and gave him an herb called the daybreak star herb. "With this on earth you shall undertake anything and accomplish it," they said. They ask him to drop it. When he did that it rooted, and grew and flowered.

The western grandfather said, "Behold all over the universe." Black Elk then saw a country full of sickness and knew in the future he was going to cure these people.

The western grandfather sang:

> Here and there may you behold.
> Here and there may you behold.
> All may you behold.
> Here and there may you behold.
> Here and there may you behold.

They had taken Black Elk all over the world and showed him all the powers. They took him to the center of the earth and to the top of the peak to view it all. This last song meant that Black Elk had indeed seen it all.

The black horse rider said, "Before you may walk back to your grandfathers you should behold a man with power."

Black Elk saw a flaming man down on the earth. He was black with horns. When he moved lightning flashed around and over his body. Around him everything was moaning and crying. Death was everywhere.

The spirits said, "Some day you shall depend upon him."

With that the man changed into a gopher standing on its hind legs. Then it changed into an herb. It looked like a little tree with crinkly leaves, reddish in color. Black Elk realized this was the soldier weed, an herb that grew in the Black Hills.[55] Nothing grew anywhere near it because it was killed immediately if it tried. Every

---

[55] Ada E. Georgia, *A Manual Of Weeds* (Macmillan, 1914), 124-125, Fig. 77: Amaranthus Spinosus, also known as Soldier Weed, Prickly Careless Weed and Spiny Pigweed.

animal that neared it died. Around where it grew there were always many skeletons. It was so destructive it could be used in war and could destroy a nation.

The western grandfather said, "Behold your herb; with it all the world will tremble. There will be disputes, and then you must depend upon the herb."

Suddenly Black Elk noticed he was painted red and all his joints were black. There was a white stripe between the joints all over his body. And whenever he breathed, lightning shot out. His bay horse had lightning stripes on it. The horse's mane was like clouds.

Black Elk had received the power of a great warrior.

Now he was to walk back to his grandfathers. He saw the rainbow flaming with the six grandfathers sitting there. He had seemed to be traveling with them, but then he found instead that he was traveling toward them. Then he saw the first two men of his vision, but they had turned into geese. The geese were in four formations flying in circles, one over each of the four directions.

The geese sang:

> In four circles they are flying
> In a sacred manner.
> May you behold them.

The western grandfather said, "Behold them, for they shall have a sacred voice for you." Here Black Elk was presented with the power of the goose voice.

As Black Elk encountered the grandfathers they cheered for him and the lightning, birds, beasts and men all cheered for him. Many voices were cheering. Some said: "He has triumphed!" All the grandfathers were sitting with their arms and palms out and said: "He has triumphed!" Black Elk could see nothing but millions of faces behind the grandfathers trying to see him. The western grandfather, pointing to all the people trying to see Black Elk, said, "Behold your nation!"

At one point the northern grandfather presented him with a cup of water. In the cup was a man painted blue holding a bow and arrow but the man was in distress. The grandfathers commanded Black Elk to drink it. When Black Elk drank it, he received not only healing power for others but for himself. When he drank it the blue spirit was a blue fish.[56]

---

[56] In later years Black Elk, while performing as a pejuta wicasa, could actually spit this blue fish (blue man/blue spirit) into a cup of water.

After some time Black Elk seemed to descend more and more to earth. Soon he saw his own tipi. As he entered the tipi he saw a boy lying there dying. He stood there awhile before he realized that he was watching himself.

Next he heard someone saying: "The boy is feeling better now, you had better give him some water." It was his mother and father stooping over him. They were giving him some medicine but that was not what cured him. It was the vision that cured him. The first thought that came to him was that his father and mother didn't seem to know that he had been gone. They didn't look glad. Black Elk felt very sad over that.

Chapter 4

AMONG THE ENEMY NEAR FORT ROBINSON

Black Elk felt he was not the same boy after he recovered from his vision. His father felt the same way and he told that to the family of 13-year-old Standing Bear.[57] Black Elk was too serious for a nine-year-old and now he liked to be alone. Black Elk felt his mother and father were not pleased with him.

Standing Bear's uncle was Whirlwind Chaser, the medicine man who had 'cured' Black Elk. Whirlwind Chaser came to see Black Elk after the recovery. Black Elk, summoned, entered the tipi and sat down. Whirlwind Chaser was surprised and very suspicious.

"Your son is sitting in a sacred manner," he told Black Elk's father. "It seems he has some special duty to do. When he came in I saw the power of lightning all through his body."

Black Elk revealed nothing.

The memory of the vision was pleasant at first but Black Elk kept silent about it. The only one he liked to be with was his grandfather Keeps His Tipi. He knew his grandfather really liked him but he could not even tell him about the vision. The vision was hard to understand. At first it was like being awakened from a dream that the dreamer felt he understood. But on reflection he realized he could not understand the dream. Did he have some special duty? It seemed a burden. Soon Black Elk didn't want to think about it.

His mysterious illness and sudden recovery might have caused more gossip than it did but just two days after he was up walking around again, the village was breaking camp to follow the buffalo.

Standing Bear sought out Black Elk during the move. Boys of Black Elk's age were near the rear of the procession. Standing Bear rode up to Black Elk, who was riding a bay pony.

"Younger brother, after all that, are you well?"

Black Elk answered, "Yes, I'm not sick at all now."

Standing Bear was impressed by Black Elk's serious demeanor. He acted much older than the other boys around him who were playing their rough, irreverent games.

---

[57] DeMallie, 143-144.

BLACK ELK

On the journey the Wakicunsas occasionally allowed the women to stop to dig for roots called 'tipsila' by the Lakotas. The plant bloomed bright purpley blue from May through July, so it was very easy to find. It was an important source of food. Just a few inches below ground the root swelled into a very edible 'turnip'. It tasted like a bean and could be eaten raw or cooked. It could also be dried, bundled together and stored. Temporarily stopping a migration for buffalo to dig for the 'tipsila' showed how important it was.

Black Elk soon became even less interesting as a subject for gossip. After the band of Big Road finally stopped to camp at their new location the village scouts reported several herds of buffalo not far away. Within minutes the village crier was yelling over and over, "Sharpen your knives. Sharpen your arrows. Get ready, hurry, get your horses ready. We will make plenty of meat!" Rich fat meat! The village buzzed with high expectations.

Buffalo were called 'wasichu'. So were the white people. Black Elk asked his grandfather Keeps His Tipi about that odd thing. His grandfather said he didn't know the answer. But Black Elk had a sick feeling 'wasichu' meant something that seemed to have no end, something too numerous to comprehend. The buffalo were like that. Were the white people like that? Were they a sea of snow-faced men coming to the land of the Lakotas?

A 13-year-old like Standing Bear went on the buffalo hunt. That age was not far from manhood for a Lakota. On the other hand, a nine-year-old like Black Elk was still learning to ride and shoot his arrows. Black Elk knew the procedure. The akicita led the procession of warriors on horses, often 20 side by side. Hunters followed in smaller groups, the foremost often hand-picked by the advisors or main councilors of the village. The hunters wore only a robe fastened at the waist. When the action started they would throw the robe back and load the bow from a quiver on their left. They rode up on the left side of a buffalo and shot the arrow into it just behind the left shoulder. That arrow had a good chance of hitting its heart and the beast soon went crashing down. The hunter yelled, "Oo-hee!" so others would know one went down. Soon not only the hunters were butchering the fallen buffalo but old people and women who followed the hunt even on foot. It was important that everyone in the village got meat. Anybody helped who was able.

They first stripped the animal of its hide, trying to leave very little meat on it.[58] They butchered so as not to cut large muscles across the grain. Doing otherwise caused problems later when the meat was cut in strips to dry. They threw the hide fur-down on a pony. Large chunks of meat were loaded on that hide, keeping the load balanced. Then the hide was thrown up over the meat to protect it. The load was taken carefully back to the village where the women would spend days processing it.

Black Elk and the boys his age at this time would meet the returning hunters and try to get pieces of raw liver to eat. He and the boys later declared war on their village. They built their own war lodges away from the village and crept up on the village to steal meat off the drying racks and have secret feasts. Black Elk climbed a tree to reach down to the top of a rack and steal a particularly appetizing tongue. But he fell to the ground and started crying. "Someone is afraid," commented a man dryly. If there was a dance the boys would flip stinging mudballs at people. They also liked to shoot dogs with blunt arrows. All this took Black Elk's mind off the vision and soon he was like the other boys again.

In the summer the Lakotas always tried to get all seven council fires together in their totality. They had a great Sun Dance and attended to matters that governed their nation. The Sun Dance itself was a grueling test of endurance for the participants and rigorously prescribed. It could be performed only in June or July during a full moon.[59] Lakota men did it to fulfill a vow made at a time of great danger or to secure supernatural powers for themselves or someone else. There was extensive preparation requiring several days for the participants, who had to cleansed and purified. They danced around a stout pole of cottonwood from the top of which they were fastened by rawhide thongs. The thong was pegged through the skin of their chests. The ordeal could be heightened by also pegging a thong to their back that dragged one or more buffalo skulls across the ground. Staring up into the sun was also agonizing. Most excruciating was being lifted by the thongs until the skin ruptured. The dance ceremony lasted days.

Leadership of the entire Lakota circle was also addressed. During the summer meeting of the Lakota all power rested in four Wakicunsas (also 'Pipe Owners'), who were not chiefs but well-

---

[58] Butchering and packing from Luther Standing Bear, *My Indian Boyhood* (1931), 45-48.

[59] Joseph Epes Brown, *The Sacred Pipe* (Un. Oklahoma, 1953), 67.

respected warriors selected by the tribal council of chiefs. The Wakicunsas enforced their decisions through one of the soldier societies selected to act as akicitas. When the great circle broke up for the winter, each council fire or camp resumed its normal way of governing: by tribal council.[60] The council was composed of the chief and elderly men of 'good repute, knowledge, and experience'. The council considered and decided upon all matters of common interest to the council fire or camp. Their appointed crier, or herald, went through the camp proclaiming decisions. The Wakicunsas enforced decisions with the help of the akicitas and settled disputes.

Even the loafers and agency Lakotas tried to join the great summer meet, usually west of the Black Hills somewhere on the four rivers, the Bighorn, the Rosebud, the Tongue and the Powder. Black Elk and his relatives had begun to consider their great Lakota nation comprised of six council fires but they were not the traditional seven Teton council fires. Of course the Oglalas, Hunkpapas, Minneconjous and Brules remained council fires, but the fifth combined the three smaller council fires of the Sans Arcs, Blackfeet and Two Kettles into one. The sixth council fire, was now not too surprisingly the powerful Cheyennes.[61]

Big Road usually stayed close to the Oglala band led by Crazy Horse. They also ran with the Minneconjous and the wildest of the Cheyennes led by Medicine Man and later Two Moons. For a while they also stayed close to the Oglala chief Red Cloud, who had terrorized the Bozeman Trail. After Red Cloud left, the Minneconjous, the Cheyennes and the Oglalas of Crazy Horse and Big Road began to associate with the Hunkpapas led by Black Moon and Sitting Bull. This association the white people called the 'Northern Indians' and they considered them the most hostile of all Native Americans on the plains. They had been very active the summer of 1873, fighting unwelcome intruders from south of the Platte River to north of the Yellowstone River.

Yet before the winter of 1873 came Big Road's band parted ways. Big Road had heard good things of a new development for the Oglala Lakotas southeast of the Black Hills and he wanted to know more about it. Red Cloud had 'untied his pony's tail'. He was trying to live peacefully with the white people. Since 1871, Red Cloud and

---

[60] pages 74-75 in James R. Walker, "The Sun Dance and Other Ceremonies of the Oglala Division of the Teton Dakota." in *American Museum of Natural History, Anthropological Papers* 16, pt. 2 (1917): 50-221.
[61] DeMallie, 140.

his Oglalas had their own 'agency' near White Clay Creek where it emptied into the White River. The White River flowed to the northeast through badlands, eventually reaching the mighty Missouri River. Forty miles northeast of the Red Cloud Agency was the agency for Spotted Tail, the chief of the Brule Lakotas.

Winter was hard on the Lakotas no matter how well prepared they were - it could turn unpredictably deadly too - and Big Road had heard of the bounty at the Red Cloud Agency. Out of fear, the Lakotas reasoned, the white people lavished gifts upon the Lakotas. The Lakotas did not consider the gifts handouts at all but the bounty of war. Tribute. The bounty was staggering:

> ...fine Indian blankets; cases of blue Indian cloth, scarlet, prints, Melton cloth, blue drill and even canvas for lodge covers; shirts, socks, coats, pants, and hats; camp kettles, axes; beef, pork, bacon, flour, coffee, sugar and tobacco....[62]

To increase the bounty the shrewd Lakotas moved back and forth between the two agencies to double-dip. The agents could not keep track of who belonged where, especially with the new faces of 'Northern Indians' coming into the agencies. Surplus gained by the Northern Indians could be used to trade for ammunition. Kettles could be used to make metal arrow heads. What a bounty gushed from the two agencies.

But not everyone thought the agencies were a good thing. The Lakotas knew some white men they thought they could trust. These white men were the traders and also the husbands of Lakota women, some called derisively 'squawmen'. These friendly white men had warned the Lakotas not to allow themselves to be pushed far north of their agency on the Platte River into agencies on the White River. That was too close to their precious Pehe Sapa (Black Hills), which the bad white men wanted.[63] And sure enough, the two agencies were by 1873 on the White River.

All Black Elk remembered of that fall trip was that the Big Road band gradually moved east toward the Red Cloud Agency and their Oglala relatives had good bread and very sweet coffee!

Eventually the Big Road Oglalas were camped on War Bonnet Creek. There the Big Road band stayed, but about 20 tipis including Black Elk's family journeyed one more day to set up camp close to the Red Cloud Agency. They set up their tipi right next to a relative,

---

[62] Hyde, *Red Cloud's Folk*, 192.
[63] Hyde, *Red Cloud's Folk*, 206.

who was Black Elk's aunt. This was the first time Black Elk had seen a white man. Some were dressed in blue coats and he heard they were the soldiers of the white men. Some soldiers wore blue pants with yellow stripes. These the agency Oglalas said fought on horses. Others wore blue pants with white stripes. The agency Oglalas said these fought on foot. Although the blue-coated soldiers were not very numerous Black Elk was alarmed. It was like wandering into a camp of Crows or Shoshones. So these were the bluecoats his own Lakotas fought sometimes. Some of the bluecoats were very large men. But so were some of his own Lakota warriors. And he knew some of the greatest Lakota warriors like Crazy Horse were not large at all. But all the soldiers seemed to have nice shiny guns too.

After a while Black Elk realized that his Lakotas greatly outnumbered the bluecoats. In fact the number of Lakotas at the agency seemed as much as the number of Lakotas at the great summer gathering. Thousands. Some said eight thousand. And his relatives said there were many lodges of Cheyennes and Arapahoes there too. After a while Black Elk lost his fear of the blue-coated soldiers. It was a good thing because they stayed all winter at the Red Cloud Agency. He would especially remember sliding down snowy hills on sleds made from the ribs of buffalo bound together with rawhide. On the ice the boys used little whips to send a top spinning into an area their opponents tried to protect.

In the moon of the Dark Red Calf, or the month of February, the 'Northern Indians' got very restless. One party of over 100 Minneconjou warriors killed two bluecoat foot soldiers with a wagon train hauling wood to Fort Laramie. On the Niobrara River warriors killed a teamster named Gray and on the Laramie Fork a man named King. The Red Cloud Agency was not spared.[64] Worried Agent Saville had turned the agency into a stockade, complete with heavy gate that was closed at night. One night[65] a warrior from Lone Horn's Minneconjou camp piled some lumber against the stockade wall and leaped into the enclosure. He intended to shoot Agent Saville dead with a pistol when he answered the door. But an agency clerk, Frank Appleton, opened the door. The warrior shot him dead. Oglalas around Black Elk thought the killer was Kicking Bear, an Oglala who ran with the Minneconjous. Black Elk's family

---

[64] Hyde, *Red Cloud's Folk*, 211-212.
[65] February 9, 1874.

had a very good idea about his involvement because they were related to Kicking bear, who was a cousin of Crazy Horse too.

The killing had major consequences.

President of the United States was Ulysses Grant. General of the Army was William Tecumseh Sherman. Philip Sheridan was Sherman's general over the area of plains in which the Lakotas lived. These three men had practiced total war without mercy against white people in the southern states. The killing at the agency was the final excuse they needed to unleash the military. Pacifists had no hope of stopping it. Within days General John E. Smith was on the march from Fort Laramie. It was no small detachment. He took six companies of cavalry and eight companies of foot soldiers. Over 1000 soldiers were heavily armed and expecting to fight.

General Smith camped at the Red Cloud Agency. With the agent's help Smith notified the Lakota chiefs the soldiers had orders to shoot if any Lakotas challenged them.

Criers spread the news through the Indian camps. "Do not go near the white soldiers! They will shoot if any Lakota comes too near!"

What hot-blooded warrior could resist that? Some rode up to the sentries and attempted to provoke them. It was a miracle fighting did not break out.

The Northern Indians did not like the odds. They moved north. But the incident of the killing was not going to blow over. The bluecoats camped one and a half miles from the agency. They called their site Camp Robinson, naming it for one of the victims killed in the wagon train hauling wood to Fort Laramie. Soon they began building houses of wood and brick. It was an ominous development. There would be a permanent intrusion of enemy soldiers only a two-day ride from the precious Black Hills. And already over 1000 heavily-armed soldiers were there in Camp Robinson.

In the moon when the Ponies Shed (month of May) the small group with Black Elk that broke off Big Road's band the previous winter broke camp and headed north. Now they had 30 tipis. They camped on Horsehead Creek between the Black Hills and Slim Butte. It was there Black Elk heard the sharp whistle of an eagle. Suddenly he wondered if that eagle was the one in his vision, which was supposed to be guarding him. He wondered if the Lakotas around him were the nation in his vision. He became acutely aware of his vision again and every time he saw a cloud he thought it might be the spirits coming to him. Maybe he was supposed to be doing something for the Lakotas. But what?

Soon they were camping at Buffalo Gap by Black Hills. Black Elk went hunting with his father. They rode up a large hill and looked down on the Cheyenne River. His father told him to wait while he drove deer toward him.

Black Elk got a queer feeling, like he was entering his vision. He said, "No father, stay here. They are bringing them toward us. We'll get them right here."

They? His father looked at him questioningly. "All right, son, but take the horses back out of the way."

His father lay down in the grass with his rifle. Black Elk stood back holding the horses. Black Elk could see forms approaching but they were not deer. They were pronghorns. Two shots rang out. He hoped his father had bagged two of the pronghorns.

When they went to the site there four dead pronghorns!

As his father butchered, Black Elk ate warm liver and kidneys. After a while he felt bad they had to kill the four animals. "Father, shouldn't we offer one of these pronghorns to the wild things?"

His father again looked at him questioningly but agreed.

They lay one of the pronghorns facing east.

His father said, "Hey-a-a-a", four times.

Then his father turned to the west, raising his hands higher.

> Grandfather, the Great Spirit, behold me.
> To all the wild things that eat flesh,
> This I have offered that my people may live
> and the children will grow up in abundance.

As they started back to camp with the meat of three pronghorns loaded on the horses Black Elk heard the eagle again and hoped it would eat some of the pronghorn. From that day on, Black Elk knew thunderstorms were coming before anyone else. He could hear a rumbling noise in the earth as he walked along. He was glad to see a storm although he knew how dangerous the thunder beings could be.

Later, when they camped at Rapid Creek they ventured into the forest to cut many straight lodgepole pines. When they brought them back they trimmed and dressed them for tipi poles. Then they built a sweat lodge for a medicine man by the name of Chips. He was renowned because he was the one who prepared Crazy Horse for war with sacred ornaments and gopher dust. Crazy Horse was considered bullet-proof.

While Black Elk was playing with boys away from camp he heard a voice urge, "Go at once."

When he returned he heard that while Chips was in the sweat lodge he had also heard a voice tell them to move out. Now the whole camp was on the move. Later they heard that the flamboyant bluecoat George Custer had led many troops into the Black Hills to protect an expedition looking for the yellow and white metals. Perhaps those prowling bluecoat soldiers with their shiny guns had been the reason for the warning.

They broke camp nearly at sunset and hurried back toward the Red Cloud Agency. They took a back trail down Spring Creek. By morning they reached the south fork of the Cheyenne River. By evening they were back on Horsehead Creek. By the second morning they were camped near the Red Cloud Agency.

They told the agency Lakotas about the bluecoat soldiers in the Black Hills. The agency Lakotas said the bluecoat soldiers were in the Black Hills to drive the gold-diggers out. None of the 'Northern Indians' believed that. There was a treaty with the whites signed by the Lakotas that assured them no whites would trespass into the Black Hills. The Lakotas knew by now the whites trespassed everywhere. Nothing escaped the greedy eyes of the whites.

In the moon of the Changing Seasons (month of October) there was another incident at the Red Cloud Agency. Agent Saville decided to erect a flagpole inside the agency stockade. Was he going to fly the United States flag over the agency or was he going to have a way to signal the soldiers at Camp Robinson? Either way the Lakotas were furious. The flagpole still lay on the ground. More and more angry Lakotas arrived at the agency. Sharp eyes could have seen they were painted and carried weapons. They summoned Agent Saville. He stepped outside. The Lakotas had waited so he could see what they were going to do. They rushed the flagpole. They hacked it to pieces with their tomahawks and axes.

Saville angrily sent a messenger to Camp Robinson. Lieutenant Emmet Crawford and 26 cavalry soldiers were sent to the agency. But Crawford was appalled to see hundreds of Lakotas riding madly toward the Red Cloud Agency. Soon hundreds were yelling war-cries and circling the bluecoats. One shot and there would have been a bloodbath.

Suddenly other Lakotas broke through the circle and began brandishing warclubs. It was Young Man Afraid of His Horse, head-soldier of the Oglala akicitas. After a while, with a harangue from Old Man Afraid of His Horse, the akicitas managed to drive the angry Lakotas off. The bluecoats were bitter about the agent's poor judgment. But the skirmish was over. There would certainly be no flagpole.

Another form of rapacious greed by whites appeared at the Red Cloud Agency the very next moon, that of the Falling Leaves (month of November), in the year 1874. Though warned of the tension at the agency Yale professor O. C. Marsh arrived - short, fat and loud - with a company of foot soldiers from Fort Laramie. There was something at or near the agency that he wanted very badly. In fact, the existence of the booty Marsh coveted had been known by whites since the 1840s. F. V. Hayden wrote condescendingly in 1869 that "Detached from the neighboring soft and readily disintegrating rocks, the fossils lie strewn about, and have often attracted the attention of the least curious of those who have traversed the district. The stone heads and turtles have even excited the wonder of the Indian."

Lakotas, who tracked animals and men so thoroughly, routinely studied the ground. What Lakota would not recognize a horse skull? Or just horse teeth. Even boys like Black Elk most certainly wondered about the other 'bones', so numerous and so obviously turtles or colossally large grazing four-legs. The pink and gray mudstone hills of the badlands around the White River were littered with the shiny tan or brown or bluish remains. Most common were teeth, some larger than a man's fist.

Hayden had noted giddily that "facilities which will soon be afforded for travel through those wild regions, on the completion of the Pacific Railroads, must give a very great impulse to explorations." [66] And here in 1874 was Marsh with a company of bluecoats, ready to begin the plunder. Some of the Lakotas were impressed. Was this man going to explain the sacred meaning of the ancient giants in the rock? Not every Lakota welcomed him. In a council called to allow Marsh access to the badlands the Oglala chief White

---

[66] quotes from pages 9-10 in F. V. Hayden, "On the Geology of the Tertiary Formations of Dakota and Nebraska." in *Journal of the Academy of Natural Sciences of Philadelphia*, v. VII, second series, 1869. Hayden had the pompous title 'geologist-in-charge of the United States Geological and Geographical Survey of the Territories'.

Tail, protested angrily. Marsh was just a gold thief whose real intention was to slither quietly into the Black Hills![67] Soon other Lakotas realized Marsh was escorted by bluecoats and intended to load several wagons with what he found. They were more than unhappy. They were ready to put on the paint and tie up their ponies' tails.

The agency trader Deer told Marsh just how to placate the Lakota chiefs. Marsh hosted a feast of copious meat, rice, and dried apples for 50 chiefs. He seemed to win over Red Cloud. The reason for Red Cloud's approval would only be evident later. Red Cloud could restrain the Oglalas for a while but Marsh was warned to avoid the Minneconjous in the badlands to the north. Minneconjous could not be placated. Marsh proceeded into the badlands at night, found an area very rich in fossils, loaded two tons - yes, 4000 pounds - of fossils into the wagons and came out one day before the Minneconjous came looking for him.

Before Marsh left with his plunder of fossils Red Cloud showed him the rations being issued by the agency to the Oglalas. The rations were abominable: flour tainted with white badlands dirt, bad coffee, moldy tobacco and spoiled pork. Red Cloud took Marsh to a nearby corral to show him lame and emaciated cattle.[68] Red Cloud hoped Marsh was grateful enough for the bone harvest to complain to the powers in Washington, D.C. about the miserable and inadequate rations given to the Lakotas.

The winter of 1874 and 1875 was bitter. But the most bitter news came when the Oglala and Brule buffalo hunters who returned from the Republican River area to the south. They barely found enough buffalo to feed themselves, let alone bring supplies for the villages.

The precious buffaloes were nearly gone![69]

---

[67] Hyde, *Red Cloud's Folk*, 225.
[68] Hyde, *Red Cloud's Folk*, 227. The rations had been spoiled by confederates of Red Cloud. The cattle had been rejected and set aside by the agency.
[69] Hyde, *Red Cloud's Folk*, 229.

Chapter 5

LAKOTAS AT WAR 1875 - 1876

Buffalo feed into the wind and the seasonal weather drove them in great circles.[70] There were four colossal herds that overlapped, some said. They moved generally north in spring and summer, then south in fall and winter. Lakotas preferred to hunt at the edges where smaller herds broke off the main herd. Few animals were tougher with fewer enemies. The buffalo was the salt of the earth.

But three things changed their stolid existence. One was the building of several east-west railroads. Another was rifles that shot cased bullets by the score. The third was the infamous hide men. Like two-legged wolves these whites came in and shot buffalos until the rifle barrels got too hot to continue. All the hide men considered themselves too good for the job, apologizing that they just wanted to make money fast and get out.

They stripped the beasts of their hides. The hides and robes were railroaded east. In 1876 dressed-out robes brought one dollar to the seller. The more the hunters diminished the herds, the scarcer the hides and robes became - and ironically, the more valuable they became. There was no economic incentive for a hide man not to shoot that very last buffalo.

The bones were also gathered and shipped east to be converted into phosphate for fertilizing. Uncrushed bones sold for about $12 per ton at their destination.

The meat was left to rot. "Probably not more than one one-thousandth of the buffalo meat that might have been saved and utilized was saved."[71]

What seemed inexhaustible - 50 million or so hardy beasts - was disappearing from the earth.

No buffalo had been found along the valley of the Platte River since 1870. By the winter of 1874 and 1875 the great buffalo herds south of the Platte River were nearly gone. North of the Platte River

---

[70] Mari Sandoz, *Buffalo Hunters: the story of the hide men* (Un. Nebraska Press, 1954) and William T. Hornaday, *The Extermination of the American Bison* (U.S. National Museum Report, 1889).

[71] Hornaday, 446.

the once vast herds were fast shrinking. The Lakota chiefs had no illusions. They knew what was happening. It was more important than ever to keep the whites out of Lakota country.

Black Elk in the summer of 1875 turned twelve. He and his family had been camped near the agency since the previous winter. The talk among the Oglala camps was that in late summer a commission of white men from the white men's government in the east would meet with the Lakotas at the Red Cloud Agency to discuss leasing the Black Hills. Lakotas like Black Elk's family expected nothing to come of it. Was anyone going to discuss it with Crazy Horse and his Oglalas? Or with Sitting Bull and his Hunkpapas?

Crazy Horse was not one to talk. He fought. Sitting Bull fought too but he also liked to talk. He sent a message to the commission:

> Are you the Great God that made me, or was it the Great God that made me who sent you? If He asks me to come see him, I will go, but the Big Chief of the white men must come see me. I will not go to the reservation. I have no land to sell. There is plenty of game here for us. We have enough ammunition. We don't want any white men here."[72]

Lone Horn of the feared Minneconjous was actually at the meeting. He attacked the Oglala Red Cloud, "You are not the only Lakotas. Raise your heads up and look over to the north and to the west. Our people are out there roaming the country and hunting buffalo. My own Minneconjous are still out there. We should wait until they are all here together."[73]

Even Spotted Tail, suspected of being as accommodating to the whites as the Oglala Red Cloud, protested. But it was weak. He merely wanted to get a better deal out of leasing the Black Hills.

Some of the whites hinted that the Lakotas had better get whatever they could because the whites were going to take the Black Hills from them anyway.

And in the summer of 1875 right in the middle of the Black Hills were many white men picking at the rocks and making maps.[74]

---

[72] Bourke, 246.

[73] paraphrased from several versions of Lone Horn's protest in DeMallie, 169-172.

[74] Henry Newton, Walter P. Jenney, et al., *Report on the Geology & Resources of the Black Hills of Dakota* (Washington, D.C.: Government Printing Office, , 1880), reports the findings of their 1875 geological expedition. Scarcely noticed by anyone in the report is the remark on page 5 that the farming

BLACK ELK

These were no grubby prospectors who sneaked into the Black Hills. They were geologists and topographers sent there by the white men in Washington, D.C., the same men who pretended to negotiate in good faith to lease the Black Hills. Furthering the affront was the presence of many bluecoated soldiers, nearly 500. They were both horse soldiers and foot soldiers, under the command of Lieutenant Colonel Richard Dodge.[75] The expedition also consisted of 71 wagons and over 100 head of cattle.

Black Elk and his family felt good about breaking camp and heading off to join Crazy Horse on the Tongue River. Whenever there was trouble Lakotas wanted to be near Crazy Horse. Even some Loafers, the people who lived around the agency, came with them. As the party skirted the Black Hills it was chance for Black Elk to go into the hills alone and seek a vision. The spirits told him at last that the duty he was to do would come to him.

When they camped on the way to the Tongue River their scouts found buffalo and they stopped to hunt for ten days. The hunt was bountiful. Then, as they broke camp to push on, the Loafers from the agency got nervous about joining Crazy Horse who they heard was very close now. The Loafers headed back to the agency.

When Black Elk's party reached Crazy Horse's large camp Black Elk was greeted - arms over each other's shoulders - by his uncle Iron Crow. But his second cousin, the great warrior, was not there. Crazy Horse roamed a lot, always gathering information and very often killing. In the camp an incident took place that deeply affected Black Elk. The Oglalas there had many horses, so many horses they had tipis by the night-time corrals. Inside the tipis were guards. Scouts had had seen Crows in the area, so guards were alert. Crows were very daring horse thieves. For all Black Elk knew Crazy Horse was out looking for the Crows.

Then one day the herald cried, "The Loafers from Red Cloud Agency have all been killed."

The Loafers had been on their way back to the agency. Although they saw the tracks of the Crows they camped and went to bed. The Crows jumped them that night and killed them all in their beds. Even two Loafers who had left the camp to gather wood were

---

possibilities on the 'Sioux Reservation' "may practically be considered as nothing". Yet for decades the government was determined to turn the Lakotas into farmers.

[75] Richard Irving Dodge, *The Black Hills Journals of Colonel Richard Irving Dodge* (Un. Oklahoma Press, 1996).

jumped and killed. Only a scout, who had not been in camp, was lucky enough to escape. That's how the camp of Crazy Horse learned what happened.

Black Elk was jumpy knowing their dreaded enemy was in the area. One night he couldn't sleep. Sure enough he heard gunshots. Lakotas started yelling that a Crow horse thief had been shot. By the time Black Elk reached the corral it was a horrific sight.[76]

The Crow had not only been scalped but ripped apart and his torso, arms and legs scattered. All the men and boys took sticks and couped him. To be among the first to coup him was a distinction. The greatest distinction of course went to the one who killed him, who was not allowed to coup. When Black Elk arrived there was already a considerable pile of coup sticks.

They had built a fire by the body, to dance and sing kill songs.

Crow Nose, who had killed the Crow, sang:

> Yellow Shirt, come forth, I have got him.
> All you have to do is coup him.

But singers honored Yellow Shirt, who had the first coup:

> Yellow Shirt, he whose heart for greatness is known

While all this dancing and singing was going on the body parts were propped up and shot full of bullets and arrows. The grisly celebration lasted all night.

That very next morning the herald came around crying that they were going to break camp. Crow Nose painted his face black and wore bear claws. He rode the horse that the unfortunate Crow had tried to steal.

The bluecoats were also prowling about the area, although they did not find the abandoned camp of Crazy Horse until a few months later. The sight was still gruesome. The officer, John Bourke, recorded it in March 1876.

> we came across a ghastly token of human habitancy, in the half-decomposed arm of an Indian, amputated at the elbow-joint, two fingers missing, and five buckshot fired into it. The guides conjectured that it was part of the anatomy of a Crow warrior who had been caught by the Sioux in some raid upon their herds and cut limb from limb.[77]

---

[76] DeMallie, 166-167.
[77] John Bourke, *Campaigning with Crook*, 268.

This was confirmed by the Grabber, Frank Grouard.

> We found where they had killed a Crow Indian, quartered him and hung him up. It was on Tongue river just below the mouth of Hanging Woman. His arms, legs, head and everything were hung up in different places on the trees down where the village had been...I heard the Indians had killed a man there in camp. He was stealing horses. It must have been done a month before. There is nothing left of a horse thief after the Indians catch him.[78]

The bluecoats were very dangerous now. Grouard had gone over to them as a scout. He had lived with Sitting Bull and Crazy Horse. He was very shrewd and a very good scout. He knew the terrain like a Lakota. And he had other knowledge. He knew where the great chiefs liked to camp. He had informants among the Loafers and other Lakotas that moved back and forth from the hunting grounds to the agency. The fact that Grabber had gone over to the whites also meant he had decided the Northern Indians were in dire trouble. He was an uncanny opportunist.

The bluecoats sent out a chilling message: Any Lakotas that did not return to the Red Cloud Agency by the beginning of the moon of the Dark Red Calf (month of February) would be considered hostile by well-armed bluecoats. That very month Black Elk and his family broke camp with a small group and headed to the Red Cloud Agency. Of course Crazy Horse did not go, but stayed with his large, well-provisioned camp.

Perhaps Black Elk's father did not like what he was hearing at the agency because they soon headed back to Crazy Horse at the beginning of summer. It is also a possibility Black Elk's family was running ammunition for the Northern Indians because many of the Lakotas that moved back and forth from the hunting grounds to the agency were involved in that activity.[79]

At War Bonnet Creek their scouts spotted a wagon train rumbling into the Black Hills. People in the wagon train shot at the scouts. An important Oglala warrior, Little Big Man, directed an

---

[78] In Joe de Barthe, *Frank Grouard* (1894), 183-184. This also shows that Grouard had very good information about the Northern Indians.

[79] Grouard in De Barthe, 118: "I was with the Northern Indians, called the hostile Indians, and they never went into the agency, but the agency Indians would come to us. They were a kind of go-between. All our ammunition was supplied by these go-betweens."

attack on the wagons. Impulsively, Black Elk and his cousin Jumping Horse joined the warriors. Black Elk was scared but after he started riding he felt normal. They circled the wagons, each attacker hanging on the far side of the horse and peering out under its neck. Black Elk had a six-shot revolver but he was so excited he didn't fire it. He heard bullets zinging through the air. Black Elk circled twice. The Oglalas abandoned the attack. No one was hurt on either side, not even the animals. Black Elk had thought of his vision while riding and wondered if his power kept everyone safe. He noticed he was the youngest one in the war party.

One of the Cheyennes praised Black Elk, Jumping Horse and another boy, Crab. One Cheyenne was amused and signed to these boys that they would be expected to fight from that day on.

Crab took it to heart. Just days later he was with another war party that actually fought some bluecoats. He was praised again in the attack that killed three of the bluecoats. There was lots of ominous news though. Miners looking for gold were not only sneaking into the Black Hills but they settled in large groups and were armed as heavily as the bluecoats. The miners were even building forts. There seemed a lot of skirmishes in the Lakota country now. Black Elk would be very relieved to see Crazy Horse again. With Crazy Horse he felt grounded and safe.

In about the middle of the moon of the Blooming Turnip (month of June) Black Elk and his family topped a ridge looking down unto the Rosebud River. Below them spread a colossal gathering of tipis on both sides of the river. They were close to some rock carved with ancient pictures. They had all gathered for the Sun Dance.[80] All of the seven council fires were there with a significant number of Cheyennes led by Two Moons, and a smattering of Arapahoes. Black Elk's friend Standing Bear, now about 16 years old , recalled that one morning a herald came around crying, "Brave men, be ready, for your time has come. It is your time to do your duty now to send voices up to the Great Spirit."

It was nearing the time of the Sun Dance. The gathering had scouts spread all through the countryside to detect intruders. The scouts carried mirrors and could flash warnings over considerable distances. To the boys it was just another opportunity to do mischief. The boys chewed elm leaves and flipped wads at each other.

---

[80] Information about the gathering for the June 1876 Sun Dance in the Rosebud River valley is from Standing Bear in DeMallie, 173-174, and Stanley Vestal, *Sitting Bull* (1957), 148-151.

They pricked people on their unprotected skin with blades of spear grass. They made pop guns from ash branches and popped them right in the face of unsuspecting adults. Women with babies carried bladder bags full of water for their baby. The boys would sneak up and puncture them. And of course any dog was a handy victim.

Sitting Bull, the great chief and medicine man of the Hunkpapas, had made a vow the previous year for the Sun Dance. He repeated it for his nephew White Bull, his adopted brother Jumping Bull, and chief Black Moon's son. They recalled it later for others.

> My God, save me and give me all my wild game animals. Bring them near me, so that my people may have plenty to eat this winter. Let good men on earth have more power, so that all the nations may be strong and successful. Let them be of good heart, so that all Lakota people may get along well and be happy. If you do this for me, I will perform the sun-gazing dance two days, two nights, and give you a whole buffalo.[81]

Black Moon conducted the Sun Dance. The principal dancer was Sitting Bull. The ceremony began during daylight with the virgin cutting the sacred cottonwood tree. Chiefs lugged it into the camp circle on poles. It was dedicated and decorated with symbols and offerings. They placed a buffalo skull on a square of soil smoothed for the altar and set a pipe up against a little scaffold before the skull. Black Moon administered the elaborate ritual of the Sun Dance. Then, naked to the waist, Sitting Bull began to fulfill his vow. He sat with his back against the sacred pole, his legs straight in front of him. He rested his arms on his thighs. Jumping Bull knelt beside Sitting Bull. Jumping Bull stuck a sharp steel awl into the skin of Sitting Bull's arm, lifted the skin up and cut a small chunk loose with a knife. Jumping Bull did this fifty times, then did the same thing to Sitting Bull's other arm fifty times.

All the time Sitting Bull chanted for mercy to Wakantanka, the Great Mysterious.

Then he rose and the long rawhide thongs attached to the top of the sacred pole were inserted in his chest. He dragged a skull attached to his back as he danced, dripping blood from over 100 wounds and staring up into the sun. Of course there were other dancers. After Sitting Bull danced all day, all night and well into the

---

[81] Vestal (1957), 148.

next day Black Moon decided that he had suffered enough. Sitting Bull at the age of 45 was barely able to stand.

Lying down he talked to Black Moon.

Black Moon announced the great Hunkpapa chief had a vision while dancing. He explained, "He looked up into the sun and saw soldiers on horseback coming down like grasshoppers, with their heads down and their hats falling off. They were falling right into our camp."

The Lakotas exulted. The vision of upside-down soldiers could only mean the bluecoats were attacking their camp but being killed.

Later, Sitting Bull warned, "When the bluecoats attack, kill them. Forget taking their horses and guns."

Standing Bear remembered later that right after the Sun Dance their scouts came into camp and reported bluecoats coming from the south. The criers were soon calling for everyone to break camp. The enormous gathering broke camp the next day, thronging up Ash Creek canyon to the west and stopping that night at the headwater of a creek that flowed west into the Little Bighorn River. They were going to establish camp again on the Little Bighorn. Criers that night told the thousands of travelers that the bluecoats appeared to be camping in the area they just left. The criers summoned warriors for a war party to fight the bluecoats on the Rosebud River. Standing Bear at sixteen years old was ready to go but his uncle told him not to go. Some warriors had to stay with the main camp on the Little Bighorn. The Lakotas already knew there was yet another army of bluecoats coming up the Yellowstone River and they might attack the Lakotas from the north.

Black Elk's friend Iron Hawk was just fourteen years old, only about one year older than Black Elk. He went with the war party. The war party numbered about 1000 warriors, of which 100 were Cheyennes. About half the warriors had guns. The bluecoats they would discover also numbered about 1000 but they had with them a formidable group of 260 Crows, Shoshones and Arikarees. They would also discover among the bluecoats their old nemesis Frank Grouard. The bluecoats were 15 companies of horse soldiers and five companies of foot soldiers under the command of Brigadier General George Crook. They had marched from Fort Fetterman on the Platte River. The Lakotas suspected they were the quarry between two armies of bluecoats, one to the north on the Yellowstone and now this one to the south on the Rosebud.

The Lakotas dearly loved setting traps for overeager foes and that was what they intended to do with this army of bluecoats in the Rosebud.[82] It was unlucky for the Lakotas that Grouard was with the bluecoats. He was very shrewd about Lakota ways. It was unlucky for the Lakotas that Crook had so many Crows, Shoshones and Arikarees with him. These allies of Crook may have saved the day for the bluecoats. The Lakota warparty swarmed onto the bluecoats and it was only quick reaction of the Crows, Shoshones, Arikarees and scouts that thwarted the initial charge. Grouard, who was in the middle of it, said later, "The coming together of the Sioux, Crows and Shoshones I think was the prettiest sight in the way of a fight that I have ever seen."[83]

Iron Hawk, only 14, was in the thick of the battle. He would remember an Oglala named Without a Tipi yanked off his horse by a Crow. Another great moment for Iron Hawk was watching a Lakota with a sacred ornament that made him bullet-proof. One Crow tried to coup him with a war-club but it had no effect on the Lakota. Another Crow tried to shoot him. Again, no effect. Then Iron Hawk saw a Crow dismount and prance around tauntingly. A Lakota tried to shoot him and missed. So Iron Hawk thought the Crow was bullet-proof too.

At one point Iron Hawk was caught between the bluecoats and the Crows. He heard a Lakota shout, "Take courage, it is a good day to die."[84] Iron Hawk charged into the Crows. He thought he got away but tore the hoof off his pony in some rocks. Then a Crow attacked him. A Cheyenne saved him. He fought the Crow hand to hand and killed him. The Cheyennes were very brave but they would dismount right in the middle of the fighting, cut off the arm of their victim at the elbow and take the forearm as a war trophy.[85]

---

[82] For a major battle that has drawn little attention in the 'Sioux War', there are several very good eye-witness accounts. Finerty was a newspaper man, colorful reporting but with unfortunate racist leanings. Charles King, Bourke and Anson Mills were all officers with Crook and left accounts. Frank Grouard was a scout with Crook. White Bull was a Hunkpapa at the battle. Stanley Vestal interviewed many old Lakotas who were there. The best non-contemporary account is J. W. Vaughan, *With Crook on the Rosebud* (Un. Nebraska Press, 1956).
[83] Grouard in De Barthe, 95.
[84] DeMallie, 175.
[85] Hyde, *Red Cloud's Folk*, 264, quoting 3rd Cavalry Captain Anson Mills.

At another spot Iron Hawk saw three Lakotas who had killed a buffalo. They had plopped right down and were eating meat. Iron Hawk, who was now on foot, joined them. One of the men put blood in a piece of hide and tied it over wounded leg of his pony. That way Iron Hawk could at least ride for a while after he finished eating. But one Lakota rode up and screamed at them to get back into the fight. Iron Hawk saw then that the Crows were fighting the Lakotas very hard.

They fought all day, the Lakotas constantly trying to lure the bluecoats into a deep canyon to the west.[86] It was all Grouard and the other scouts could do to keep General Crook from storming Fetterman-like into the canyon. Finally toward dusk the Lakotas withdrew. Casualties were surprisingly light for over 2000 people shooting, stabbing and hacking at each an entire day. Each side had fewer than 30 killed and 60 wounded. Black Elk probably heard when the war party returned to the great camp on the Little Bighorn that Crazy Horse did indeed have a trap set but Crook would not take the bait.

Iron Hawk made it back to camp. The next morning Standing Bear and other boys who had missed the fight went to the battlefield. The bluecoats were gone, though they had raised a cloud of dust retreating to the south. They had buried their dead and then built a fire over the spot, a trick that fooled no Lakota. The boys saw the spadework. The boys dug up the grave, which was shallow, and plundered the bodies. They took all the blankets. They cut one finger off to get a diamond ring. They took some scalps.

General Crook, invoking some archaic maxim, claimed victory because the Lakotas 'abandoned the field'. But Crook had almost immediately retreated several miles to the south, established camp on Goose Creek, hunted, fished, watched his soldiers play baseball and virtually retired his army from the campaign that was supposed to pincer the Lakotas.[87] Crook would camp there and wait for reinforcements for the next six weeks! The Lakotas were well satisfied. Even though the bluecoats did not fall into their trap, the bluecoats of Crook had removed themselves as a threat.

---

[86] According to Bourke, 311, Crazy Horse "stated afterwards...His plan of battle was [to]... draw the whole of Crook's forces down into the canyon of the Rosebud, where escape would have been impossible."

[87] James T. King, "Needed: A Re-evaluation of General Crook" in *Nebraska Historical Society*, v 45, no. 3, 223-236, makes a very good case that Crook failed.

Chapter 6

WINNING THE BATTLES BUT LOSING THE WAR

Unknown to the Lakotas at the time of Crook's defeat on June 17 and subsequent retreat was the fact that some bluecoats had left the Yellowstone River to the north, marched south and found the site of the Rosebud battle only one day or two after Crook left. Those soldiers under Major Reno noted the very obvious signs of a battle and rushed back the 50 miles to the Yellowstone River. On June 20 Reno reported to their commander, Brigadier General Alfred Terry.

Terry decided he would send part of his 1400-man army south back up the Rosebud to follow the trail of the Lakotas. This part of his army numbered 12 companies of the 7th Cavalry - with scouts and civilians, about 650 men in all - commanded by Lieutenant Colonel George Custer. With the rest of the command, about 750 horse soldiers and foot soldiers, Terry would continue west on the Yellowstone River, then head south up the valley of the Little Bighorn River. There on June 27th the two armies would attack the Lakotas from two directions. They expected to fight 800 warriors at the most, outnumbering the Lakotas nearly 2 to 1.

General Terry supposedly joked, "Don't be greedy, Custer. Wait for the rest of us."

Custer pushed hard up the Rosebud River valley. Many of his men - the 300 or so soldiers in the Reno scout party - were not well rested. Custer had with him his two brothers Boston and Thomas, his brother-in-law James Calhoun, and his nephew Henry Reed. It was nice that his family would get to witness his expert prowess against the Indians. It was likely that he began to think he had the perfect opportunity to steal the show from Terry and the rest of the army. What could 800 Lakota warriors do against 650 heavily-armed, well-disciplined soldiers?

Custer reached the site of the battle of the Rosebud on the evening of the 24th and picked up the trail left by the Lakotas that ran west to the ridge. The Lakotas were obviously going to the valley of the Little Bighorn River. So far their speculation had been perfect. Custer had only to rest his troops for a day, then cross the divide - a march of no more than one day - and be ready to attack on the 27th.

But he did not rest his troops. He went straight into an all-night march across the divide to get his troops into position.

Meanwhile, Black Elk was in the great camp along the Little Bighorn River. On the east side of the river the land rose sharply into hills. Far to the west of the river hills rose again and this slope is where the great gathering kept a pony herd of thousands. The circles of the council fires were spread north to south on the floodplain west of the Little Bighorn. Northernmost were the Cheyennes. Then came the Brules, then Minneconjous. Next were Black Elk's Oglalas, after that the most southern circle of the Hunkpapas. Other smaller Lakota council fires like the No Bows and Blackfeet were there too.

One morning, Black Elk was going to go swimming in the river with other boys when he noticed medicine men treating a wounded man in a tipi. Rattling Hawk had been shot through the hip at the fight on the Rosebud. The main medicine man was Hairy Chin. He and several of his sons were going to perform the bear ceremony. He must have known Black Elk's reputation as a boy with strange powers because he ordered him to help with the ceremony. Hairy Chin wore a bear robe with the head still on it. On his back was an eagle with spread wings. His sons were painted red and had bear ears on their heads. He painted Black Elk yellow all over and tied up his hair so it looked like ears. All the young ones also had eagle feathers on their heads.

Hairy Chin sang, "At the doorway the sacred herbs are rejoicing."[88]

Hairy Chin gave Rattling Hawk a sacred cane painted red. A woman on one side of the wounded man held a cup of water. One on the other side held an herb. The women gave these things to Rattling Hawk, who suddenly was able to stand up. The women led him out of the tipi and faced him south. All the 'bears' groaned and Black Elk saw flames shooting from them. Then Rattling Hawk began walking with the sacred cane.

The ceremony was by no means over.

Hairy Chin grabbed Black Elk, chewed an herb and blew it into his mouth. Then he threw down Black Elk, who began growling and acting like a bear. Then they all seemed like real bears to Black Elk. The bears even ate a dog raw.

---

[88] DeMallie, 178-180.

Then the exhausted Black Elk finally got to take his swim and wash off the yellow paint.

After sunset, dances were being performed all over the camp. Kill songs were being sung too. There was tension but a feeling of great strength too.

The next morning (the white men's June 25th), Black Elk and his cousin were tending their several horses. The two boys were to take them onto the slopes to the west and let them graze. His father told him to keep a long rope on one horse and to be alert. If anything happened in the camp Black Elk should mount that horse, round up the other horses and bring them back to the tipi as quickly as possible. The boys spent the morning with the ponies, then brought them all back in to water them at the river. The boys were hungry too. And they wanted to go swimming. By the middle of the afternoon Black Elk had a sick feeling that in a short while something terrible was going to happen.[89]

Suddenly Black Elk heard the crier in the Hunkpapa circle. "Chargers are attacking! Chargers are attacking!"

Next, the crier in the Oglala circle repeated the warning.

Black Elk's cousin was just bringing their horses back from the river. They were lucky because others had to run far to the pony herd for their horses. Black Elk's brother Runs in the Center grabbed his sorrel from Black Elk's cousin and was off like a flash. Black Elk's father was upset. He told Black Elk to take his brother a gun. Black Elk jumped on a buckskin and rode after him. The Lakotas were all stopped at the south edge of the Hunkpapa circle. Dust billowed up everywhere but Black Elk could see to the south and not that far away were about 100 bluecoats.[90] They were shooting at the Lakotas with short rifles called carbines. The carbines boomed. They fired a very large bullet. Black Elk seemed like he was in a dream but he found his brother. The Hunkpapa crier yelled that the bluecoats had already killed a Lakota boy.

Black Elk's brother Runs in the Center took his gun and told Black Elk to go back with the Oglalas. But Black Elk had another gun with him. It was a six-shot revolver and he intended to use it if he had to. The Lakota warriors rushed into some woods near the river for cover. Black Elk experienced one of the side effects of war. He heard bullets snicking through the trees and saw leaves drifting

---

[89] DeMallie, 180-184, relates Black Elk's story of the Battle of the Little Bighorn.

[90] Major Marcus Reno with 7th Cavalry companies A, G and M.

down. Lakotas were shouting encouragement to each other but they were holding back, waiting on their ponies. Women and children were running west into the pony herd and the hills. He remembered his vision and the memory of the Thunder Beings made him feel strong. He was sure because the Lakotas were relatives of the Thunder Beings they would defeat the bluecoats.

Then he heard Lakotas yelling, "Crazy Horse is coming! Crazy Horse is coming!"

And Crazy Horse did what every Lakota knew he would do. He and other mounted warriors charged the bluecoats. Black Elk watched in disbelief as the Lakotas clashed with the bluecoats. More and more Lakota ponies roared past the Hunkpapa circle to attack the soldiers. Black Elk could actually see hand to hand fighting. One mounted bluecoat had killed several Lakotas with his pistol.[91] But the Lakotas - now numbering in the hundreds - were getting the upper hand. The bluecoats were also trying to move into brush and trees along the river. When pressed, the bluecoats dismounted and one soldier held several horses while the other soldiers fired their pistols or carbines. Lakotas had learned it was best to first kill the one holding the horses when bluecoats dismounted. Then the Lakotas would wave blankets to try to scatter the horses, leaving the soldiers on foot. But these bluecoats were tough and disciplined.

Suddenly the bluecoats mounted. They kept fighting but were pulling back. Then they raced south, next veered east and thrashed across the river. They rode up into the bluffs over the river. Black Elk joined some other boys too young to join the warriors and the mounted boys began finding downed bluecoats. They plundered the bodies, taking guns, ammunition and some things that were unknown to them. Only later would they find out about money and watches. They tried on the bluecoat clothing.

All the fighting was taking place higher on the bluffs. Once while Black Elk sat mounted, he saw a bluecoat thrashing around on the ground near the river. A Lakota warrior told Black Elk to dismount and scalp him. Black Elk did and clumsily tried to scalp him. The bluecoat had short hair. The man was grinding his teeth, so Black Elk shot him in the forehead, then scalped him.

Soon the boys headed north back into the camp and thought they saw another battle going on a high hill far to the northeast.[92]

---

[91] The valor of Captain Thomas French made a big impression on the Lakotas. He survived the battle and died in 1882.
[92] It was Custer and his five companies being killed to the last man.

BLACK ELK

Black Elk located his mother on a hill to the west. Just as he hoped Leggins Down was thrilled by his scalp and gave him a tremolo. Other women were giving tremolos and singing. One beautiful girl sang[93]:

> Brothers-in-law, now your friends have come.
> Take courage.
> Would you see me taken captive?

Black Elk and his mother watched the dust hover over the high hills east of the river and heard the pinging of bullets and booming of guns. Once in a while they would hear the whir of a bullet that came too close to them. Warriors began to come back into camp with scalps and the big American horses. But Black Elk joined six other boys who wanted to ride back across the river to the battlefield. They saw a bunch of big gray horses that the bluecoats liked to ride. They had no riders now. They saw some bluecoats pumping their arms as if they were running. But they were only walking and being pummeled with hatchets and warclubs, which warriors always preferred to guns. It was braver and more personal.

They found bluecoats groaning and still writhing around. The boys shot arrows into these men, even if they were already dead. Or they would push arrows in deeper. Black Elk started to strip a man of his blue coat but a warrior took it from him. Then Black Elk found a beautiful disc-like ornament on a chain. Both were yellow and shiny. The disc had engraving on it. Black Elk had for himself a fine necklace.[94] Black Elk found yet another bluecoat groaning and writhing. Black Elk had shot so many of his arrows he now had only one blunt one. He shot it into the bluecoat's forehead. The man stopped groaning but his arms and legs quivered. Black Elk took another scalp but gave it to a younger boy. Lakota and Cheyenne women were now on the battlefield, doing much as the boys did.

Black Elk saw warriors tending the Oglala Black Wasichu. He had been riding the side of his horse when he was shot. The bullet went in his shoulder, then all the way down to his hip. His father and Black Elk's father took their anger out on a dead bluecoat. They butchered him. They said with grim humor his meat was fat enough to eat. The sight and smell of blood sickened Black Elk and he went back to the tipi.

---

[93] DeMallie, 183.
[94] DeMallie, 184. A pocket watch and chain.

Eventually the battle in the bluffs quieted. Not all the bluecoats were dead. A large number were dug in to the southeast and able to resist attacks. Many Lakotas and Cheyennes on the hills now were taking care of their own dead. That night the camps never slept but danced and sang kill songs. Black Elk heard much about how the battle went.

First, about 100 bluecoats came from the south shooting into the Hunkpapa circle, then were repulsed and sent retreating across the river. That first attack however caused murderous damage to some Hunkpapas. Even the boy killed south of the circle was Hunkpapa. The Hunkpapa war chief Gall lost his two wives and three children in the hail of bullets. Not far from where the bluecoats forded the river they had gone much higher on the bluff and dug in. Now they protected themselves very well. Next, more bluecoats - maybe 200 - joined the first bunch and dug in enough to defend themselves.[95]

The most exciting development was that about 300 bluecoats had tried to move north in the high bluffs east of the river so they could attack the great camp from the north. They may have tried to go down to cross the river there and failed because then they went back up to collect on a very high hill. As soon as the bluecoats that first attacked went into a retreat the rest of the great camp swarmed up after the 300 bluecoats to the north and east.

Several waves went after the bluecoats. Judging from the sounds of gunfire there were three main concentrations of fighting. At first the Lakota and Cheyenne warriors crawled up the hillside on hands and knees to exchange shots. Then some warriors found ravines from which they could fire at the bluecoats as fast as they could load their guns. But later the warriors stormed the bluecoats on their ponies. Some said this was led by Crazy Horse. No Lakota would doubt that. There was enough killing to satisfy everyone in the camp. For one day.

Black Elk heard about fifty of their own warriors died. But for a while some like Black Wasichu would die every day from deadly wounds. So eventually about 100 Lakota and Cheyenne warriors would die from the battle. The talk was that they had killed maybe as many as 300 bluecoats. The killing wasn't over either. The next morning they could all take a crack at the bluecoats who were dug in to the southeast.

---

[95] Remains of six companies under the commands of Reno and Benteen.

BLACK ELK

Out early next morning was Black Elk. Down by the river below the place where the bluecoats were dug in boys found a bluecoat hiding in bullberry bushes. He surely crawled down there for water. The boys chased him around, pelting him with arrows. Finally even the boys were disgusted with him and set fire to the bushes.

Then they crawled toward the bluecoats who were dug in. But the bluecoats were shooting at anything that moved. One could not get that close to them. Warriors were planning a charge on horseback to engage the bluecoats. It promised to be another great bloody triumph. A large number of Lakotas were around Black Elk. Even his mother was there, riding a mare. But then the main camp signaled them with mirrors. They raced back to camp with bullets from the bluecoats zinging around them.

An army of hundreds of bluecoats was approaching from the north following the Little Bighorn upstream.

All their lives the Lakotas had been trained to break camp and get moving within an hour. This day was no exception. By dusk they were on the move. Black Elk remembered in particular that he had to ride a travois with a litter of pups. All night long he had to retrieve pups and put them back on the travois.

They traveled south with few breaks, then took Wood Louse Creek into the Bighorn Mountains. They left many dead in trees and on scaffolds on their way.[96] One was Black Wasichu. Their convoy had hundreds of Lakotas. They found relief in singing kill songs.

One kill song was:

> When you came attacking,
> why did not you have more men?
> Why didn't you bring more men
> so that you would be a little stronger?

Many kill songs mocked Custer:

> Long Hair, guns I hadn't any.
> You brought me some.
> I thank you.
> You make me laugh!

---

[96] DeMallie, 196: Black Elk remembered their immediate destination as the Bighorn Mountains via Wood Louse Creek. Gall remembered fleeing to the Absaroka Mountains via Lodge Pole Creek. A possible explanation is that the bands split up after a few days of traveling to make it very confusing to follow them.

Eventually Black Elk's group worked its way back to the Rosebud River, close to the site of the recent Sun Dance, then crossed the divide to the Tongue River. At the Yellowstone River some Lakotas attacked the steamship *Far West* to steal corn. But soldiers there shot and killed the warrior Yellow Shirt, the first Oglala to count coup on the Crow horse thief.

All that fall Black Elk's family - still numbered among the camp of Big Road - stayed close to the camp of Crazy Horse, who moved around the vicinity of the Tongue River and the Powder River. In the moon of the Popping Trees (month of December) they sent a delegation of four Lakotas to bluecoat Colonel Nelson Miles, who operated a cantonment on the Yellowstone River at the mouth of the Tongue River. They would explore the possibility of peace. The delegation was intercepted and murdered by Crow scouts working for Miles. The Crows fled, so desperate they swam an ice-cold river to escape. Crazy Horse thought the soldiers had helped the Crows murder the delegates, so that ended any peace overtures. To mollify themselves the Oglalas stole 250 head of cattle from the bluecoat cantonment.

Nevertheless it was a very bad winter for the Oglalas around Crazy Horse. Even he was getting weary of their hardships, saying at times he did not care if the others went in to live at the agencies. Once, Black Elk's family found Crazy Horse camped by a creek with only his wife. It seemed a dream. The great war chief told Black Elk's father he knew others thought he was acting very strange but he had to be alone to think and allow the spirits to direct him.

As members of Big Road's camp, Black Elk's family returned to the Red Cloud Agency at the beginning of the moon when the Ponies Shed (month of May). Shortly after that Crazy Horse finally came in with his Oglalas. John Bourke witnessed it.[97]

> 'Crazy Horse' had with him not quite twenty-five hundred ponies, over three hundred warriors, one hundred and forty-six lodges, with an average of almost two families in each, and between eleven hundred and eleven hundred and fifty people all told, not counting the very considerable number who were able to precede the main body, on account of having fatter and stronger ponies...

---

[97] Both quotes that follow are from Bourke, 413.

The new arrivals surrendered their weapons. "One hundred and seventeen fire-arms, principally cavalry carbines and Winchesters, were found and hauled away in a cart. 'Crazy Horse' himself gave up three Winchesters..."

Most chiefs were very talkative, skilled at talking in a captivating way for a long time. Even the whites were anxious to hear what Crazy Horse had to say on such a momentous day.

He said, "This day I have untied my horse's tail and layed my gun aside and I have sat down."[98] And he did sit down.

Almost the very day Crazy Horse arrived at the Red Cloud Agency Sitting Bull took his Hunkpapas into Canada. The days of Crazy Horse at the Red Cloud Agency seemed too tragic for Black Elk to remember. Other chiefs were jealous of the fame of Crazy Horse with the whites. Many whites were afraid of him. Crazy Horse rarely explained himself. But he became more and more agitated by the intense hostility toward him. His behavior seemed erratic and dangerous. By the moon of the Black Calf (month of September) the many schemers and the ever bungling General Crook had arranged to try to arrest Crazy Horse. Except a warrior like Crazy Horse would not allow it. So they murdered him on the spot by stabbing him in the back and immediately everyone involved in the murder was pointing the finger at someone else who was involved.[99]

---

[98] DeMallie, 203.

[99] Black Elk did not point a finger then or later but Mari Sandoz was told on the Pine Ridge Reservation that Black Elk's family blamed Red Cloud for a controlling part of the tragedy. See Helen W. Stauffer, *Story Catcher of the Plains* (Un. Nebraska Press, 1982), 81.

Chapter 7

ESCAPE TO CANADA AND RETURN

The murder of Crazy Horse soured many of those Oglalas who had come into the agency with him. To make matters worse the American government decided every Lakota at the Red Cloud Agency must move 250 miles up to the Missouri River for any future rations or supplies.[100] Lakotas reluctantly trudged off in a great caravan in the moon of the Changing Seasons (month of October). But the Big Road band and hundreds of Lakotas including Black Elk's family broke away and fled first to the Little Missouri, next to their beloved Powder River area and then on to Canada. There they would join Sitting Bull and his Hunkpapas. Not a few had to be thinking this was what Crazy Horse should have done back in the moon of Dark Calf.

Their friends, the Cheyennes, had also surrendered in the summer of 1877 at the Red Cloud Agency, thinking they would live there with the Oglalas. But the whites had a nasty surprise for the chiefs that included Dull Knife and Little Wolf, at gunpoint packing their Cheyennes off to the completely alien Oklahoma territory. On the other hand, the Cheyenne Two Moons surrendered to bluecoat Nelson Miles at the Tongue River Cantonment and was allowed to stay in that area. It was a peculiarly unfair accommodation of the Cheyennes and reeked of future trouble.

Black Elk's family settled on Frenchman River in Canada, almost 400 miles due north of their old hunting grounds. There were far fewer redcoats in Canada than bluecoats in America. But they were nevertheless oppressive. The redcoats insisted on strict obedience to the law. They were not willing to overlook the Lakotas' love of stealing horses. And the Lakotas found the most plentiful buffalo were just south in America. This meant they were harassed for frequently crossing the border, which they considered ridiculous because it was just an imaginary line concocted by white people. And there were no rations. The Lakotas had to get their own food by hunting or by buying it from traders.

---

[100] Hyde, *Red Cloud's Folk*, 299.

To make things even more unpleasant they found that Sitting Bull was no favorite of the Canadian whites. The redcoats considered him a magnet for every unhappy warrior in America. About the time the Big Road Lakotas arrived, there arrived also a group of Nez Perce who had fled to Sitting Bull. The Canadian whites undercut the authority of Sitting Bull whenever they could and made it clear they would much prefer him south in America. Black Elk's family got the feeling that the great Hunkpapa was forced to toady to the redcoats. They even had him groveling to their greatest enemy, the Crows. And to make it worse, in Canada the Crows seemed to win most conflicts with the Lakotas.

So it was not paradise in Canada.

But there were no bluecoats.

In the spring of 1878 their scouts found buffalo. Black Elk was now approaching his 15th birthday. He was expected to be able to hunt buffalo. When he was getting his ponies ready - he would ride his bay and lead his very fast roan - he heard a voice warn him to be alert this morning. He was going to hunt with his uncle Running Horse. On the way he told his uncle he would help butcher but he could not hunt. He needed to be on the alert.

While they were butchering a buffalo killed by his uncle a voice told Black Elk to look around. His uncle felt it too. He told Black Elk to mount and ride up on a hill to look around. On the hill Black Elk saw about 60 warriors - not Lakotas, possibly Nez Perce - chasing down two buffalo hunters. The hunters were not Lakotas either but Crows and they were killed. Black Elk and his uncle cached their meat and rode back to their camp. The spirits saved Black Elk. When was he going to do something about his vision?

After a Lakota Sun Dance in the moon of the Blooming Turnip Black Elk was again hunting buffalo with his uncle. After three days they were in a camp drying a lot of meat. His uncle told him to go kill another buffalo but just to bring back the fat. While Black Elk was butchering his buffalo a thunderstorm rolled in. A voice warned him something was going to happen that day. He loaded the fat, then rushed back to the camp of his uncle and other Oglalas.

The camp loaded up and just as they crossed a creek they were attacked by Crows. Several Lakotas were killed, including his cousin Hard to Hit. Black Elk took it on himself to protect the wife of Hard to Hit. That night the two encountered ten Nez Pierce riders. Nez Perce were not always friendly but these were. They all rode to the main camp. There by custom Black Elk was obligated to wail all day for his cousin. He did it although he admitted to himself he didn't feel like it.

The following winter (1879-1880) the Lakotas in Canada had little to eat. While Black Elk was out hunting in the snowy wilds with his father he heard a coyote howl, then it seemed to talk to him. The coyote warned him that although there were buffalo nearby to the west there were also warriors nearby. Black Elk told his father.

When they hunted the next morning they found tracks of two men. When they followed them they led to two Lakotas. Yet Black Elk and his father could find no buffalo, even from a high ridge. Then as they sat with the other two in a shelter from the weather lamenting the lack of food several buffalo began to drift out of some trees. All four of the Lakotas stood and thanked the four quarters of the earth.

The two older men were to shoot and the younger ones were to ride after the buffalo. Only one buffalo went down from the guns. Black Elk and the other young man rode hard after the fleeing buffalo. The buffalo broke the hard crust of snow as they ran. Some veered into a gulch. As Black Elk followed, his pony went down. He jumped up and saw that four buffalo were in the gulch mired in deep snow. He shot all four.

He learned the other young Lakota had killed three more buffalo. Black Elk needed help freeing his hands which were frozen to the metal of his rifle. Then the other three butchered for the rest of the day. Because they had too much meat to carry back to camp they buried it and piled snow over it. The next morning the Lakotas were back to butchering. Eventually they divided the meat and packed it back to their camps.

They had exhausted five horses so much from the hunt that the horses soon died. Their other horses began to die too from lack of fodder. The famine and problems with the Canadian authorities were too much. Even Sitting Bull was close to returning to America, but he would be at the Standing Rock Agency on the Missouri. Most of his Hunkpapas, including the prominent chief Gall, had already returned to that agency.

In the moon of Tender Grass (month of April) in 1880 Black Elk headed back to the American agencies, where Lakotas were issued food to eat in the winter. At least they did not starve there. In Black Elk's traveling party were two families totaling six women and three men including medicine man Chased by Spiders. Most were on foot because they had among all of them only five horses. One night after two or three days traveling in America they camped near the Missouri River. A voice warned Black Elk to be alert. It had been a long time since he had heard a voice and he was doubting it.

He labored up high bluffs nearby. He crawled the last few yards to the crest so he would not be seen by anyone looking at the heights. He spotted two men on a bluff not far away peering down at the very camp of Black Elk! The two men carefully backed off, then ran down the hill. Black Elk was overwhelmed by his lack of faith. He prayed to the spirits; he had faith. He would depend on the power they gave him to protect the Lakotas.

He ran to camp and told them they must break camp. Enemies were about. They departed so quickly they left their tipis. As they fled, a thunderstorm developed over them. Black Elk was certain the Thunder Beings were there to protect them. He heard gunfire and was sure the enemy were firing into their tipis.

When they were safely away the sky cleared. Black Elk was convinced now he had power. Later they came to a village of Minneconjous and heard that some Blackfeet Lakotas had killed some Crows at the very campsite that Black Elk's party had fled. Black Elk was convinced more than ever he had power. But he felt bad that he had neglected his vision.

Black Elk and his party crossed the Missouri River on a steamship. Two more days on land headed a little west of south and they camped near Fort Keogh. This was the former cantonment established by bluecoat Nelson Miles on the Yellowstone River at the mouth of the Tongue River. They participated in a Sun Dance there in June. Stopping there to get supplies from Fort Keogh was a mistake though because bluecoats confronted them. Black Elk's small party lost their guns. The men were allowed to keep only two horses a piece.

They learned the Oglala and Brule agencies were back on the White River. But they were no longer called Red Cloud Agency for the Oglalas and Spotted Tail Agency for the Brules. Now they were called Pine Ridge Agency for the Oglalas and Rosebud Agency for the Brules. The Pine Ridge Agency was still located close to Fort Robinson. There was no getting away from bluecoats for Oglalas.

They learned about 300 Cheyennes of Dull Knife and Little Wolf had fled the Oklahoma territory in the moon of the Black Calf (September) in the year 1878. Their hearts were bad and they killed not only any whites who tried to stop them but killed many whites for food or horses. They fought soldiers and settlers all across Kansas and Nebraska. They had killed over 40 whites in their flight north. Then the chiefs had a falling out. Dull Knife went to the Pine Ridge Agency for the Oglalas. Little Wolf pushed north toward the Powder River country.

Dull Knife's faction discovered they had made a fatal mistake.[101] Spurred by Philip Sheridan, the army at Fort Robinson was going to take Cheyenne leaders to court trials in Kansas to be tried for murder. The rest they would march back to Oklahoma territory in January 1879, freezing weather or not. For once George Crook urged restraint. But the Dull Knife Cheyennes had learned of the intolerable plans. Yet another murderous conflict erupted. The Cheyennes fought ferociously with few weapons. At least half of the Dull Knife Cheyennes died, including women and children. Yet by the time Black Elk's family had reached Fort Keogh the surviving Cheyennes, even Dull Knife, had joined Two Moons near Fort Keogh.

After the Sun Dance near Fort Keogh Black Elk went through a very bad time. He had been feeling guilty about doing nothing about his vision. But he didn't know what to do. He had just turned 17. He had heard those who disobeyed the Thunder Beings were struck by lightning.[102] He believed it. He dreaded thunderstorms and they were common in July. Any time it stormed he could hear Thunder Beings rumbling their disappointment with him. Even birds scolded him. Coyotes or crows would call, "It is time."[103] He became very disagreeable, even with his family. What was he supposed to do about his vision? He began to fear the Thunder Beings as never before. The fear became constant. At night he ran from tipi to tipi in a vain attempt to somehow escape the Thunder Beings. He kept it up all night long.

His father who was very tolerant of Black Elk knew at last it was time to get him help.

The medicine man Black Road appeared. He had been prepared by Black Elk's father, who himself knew a great deal about visions. Black Road asked, "Did you have a vision?"

---

[101] Source for the sorry debacle: Thomas R. Buecker, *Fort Robinson and the American West, 1874-1899* (Nebraska St. Historical Society, 1999), 125-148.

[102] Clark Wissler, "Societies and Ceremonial Associations in the Oglala Division of the Teton-Dakota." Anthropological Papers of the American Museum of Natural History 11, pt. 1 (1912), 84.

[103] DeMallie, 213.

BLACK ELK

Black Elk poured out his vision. He had almost forgotten how long and detailed it was. Black Road was astonished that a nine-year-old could have had such a long, detailed vision. That usually meant the person had real power. Black Road knew what Black Elk must do.

"You must honor your vision. The bay horse said to you, 'Behold, your horses are dancing.'"

Somehow Black Elk realized he must first perform the horse dance. This surprised him because usually if someone had a vision they had to first become 'heyoka' by being contrary and clownish and absurd.[104]

Black Road wasted no time. The next morning the herald cried out that the tipis should camp in a circle around the council tipi. Then Black Road, with the help of an elder named Bear Sings, painted symbols on the council tipi from Black Elk's vision: buffalos, elks, the four quarters, the herbs and everything that Black Elk had received. They even painted a rainbow over the tipi door. Next they met with Black Elk to hear the various songs in the vision. Black Road and Bear Sings would sing these songs while Black Elk danced the horse dance. While Black Elk sang the songs for them Thunder Beings rumbled over the camp.

Black Elk and the others had to fast and be purified in a sweat lodge. Meanwhile Black Elk's family was gathering the horses he needed for the dance. It was no small task collecting the bay, four blacks, four sorrels, four buckskins and four white horses. Black Road and Bear Sings enlisted pretty maidens to be the four virgins. They gathered the flowering branch, the sacred pipe with the spotted eagle on it, bow and arrow, cup of water and various herbs. Of course they had 16 riders for the horses. And they had to decorate horses as they were in the vision. There were six elders to represent the six grandfathers. They could all sing whatever was necessary. Only people like the Lakotas who sang and danced as a way of life could have mastered the vision so quickly.

Sage was sprinkled everywhere for its pleasing aroma.

Black Elk had painted his forearms black. He held only a stick painted red to represent the sacred arrow.

Outside the tipi Black Elk began the horse dance that represented his vision. All the performers did well. Even the horses seemed to prance on cue. During the performance Black Elk showed

---

[104] Wissler (1912), 84.

his power. Around the camp a storm lashed the earth with hail and lightning flashed. Yet it never touched the camp. As Black Elk danced and the others sang, the bay horse "began to paw and stick her tail up and point her head toward where the sun goes down".[105] The horse was honoring the western grandfather and the Thunder Beings. Some of the performers seemed overcome and began dancing too.

As Black Elk was dancing out his vision he seemed to be having another vision. He saw the swallows, men in the sky, even the flowering branch began to bud. All the while thunderstorms danced around the camp. During the performance the assemblage had sang and danced around the circle of the camp four times. At last it was completed.

They couldn't wait to examine the inside of the tipi because they had smoothed all the dirt inside when the dance started. And all over that fresh dirt inside the tipi were small hoof prints. Spirit horses had danced inside the tipi during the horse dance outside the tipi.

Black Elk was elated. At 17 he was acknowledged a medicine man. The medicine men themselves now accepted him for the first time. He was no longer a boy who acted strange but a young man with power from the spirits. He seemed to see how everything was related. He could be watching a coyote and it would change into an herb. He saw all kinds of things transform into other things. They were all sacred.

Soon after the horse dance, Lakotas were deprived of their ponies and loaded onto a steamship that took them down the Yellowstone River into the Missouri River, then on to Fort Yates where the Standing Rock Agency for Hunkpapas was located. That was not at all convenient for Oglalas. Lugging all their possessions, Black Elk and three others had to trudge on foot 300 miles south to their Pine Ridge Agency.[106] On the way they camped seven times with a stopover at the Rosebud Agency for the Brules. By the time they reached the Rosebud Agency they were living on wild plums. They visited relatives at the Rosebud Agency or they may have intended to double-dip on rations. They arrived at Pine Ridge in the moon of the Black Calf (September) in the year 1881.

---

[105] DeMallie, 221.
[106] DeMallie, 232: Oglalas called Pine Ridge "Wakpamni", referring to the place of 'distribution' of government annuities.

BLACK ELK

On the way there on his trek Black Elk had climbed a hill and faced west. He sang the first song from his vision. The same two men appeared in the sky, pointing at Black Elk with their bows and arrows. He knew they wished him to perform his healing with the power the spirits had given him. He felt it was his duty to make the Pine Ridge Agency his home and help the Oglalas with his power. He could hardly wait until the time of year came again when the Thunder Beings were around. He was to perform another ceremony for the people then.

He settled at a tiny community called Manderson just one mile west of Wounded Knee Creek but many Oglalas lived along the creek. It was no coincidence that Big Road had settled on the creek too. Most of the 'Northern Indians' located in that area. Amazingly the chief Red Shirt also settled there. He had scouted for the 4th Cavalry bluecoats during all the fighting between the Oglalas and bluecoats. He was an accommodationist much like Red Cloud. Many considered him a Loafer. His nearness to one of the most hostile Oglala chiefs showed how tolerant the Oglalas could be with each other about such things.

There was a well established Lakota trail that went east from the neighborhood of Big Road to the Rosebud Agency. It was virtually the only well-traveled trail between the agencies. That same trail bent sharply south from the neighborhood of Big Road to end up at the Pine Ridge Agency where supplies were issued. Red Cloud and the longtime agency Oglalas lived right next to the supplies.

For the first time in his life Black Elk lived in a rectangular house made of logs. If the Lakotas were no longer going to follow the buffalo the extremely portable tipi was less useful. Nevertheless many Lakota customs and rituals were imbedded in tipi living. Black Elk heard there were now about 500 of these loghouses.[107] The Lakotas built the loghouses themselves. According to Pine Ridge Agent Valentine McGillycuddy, the agency furnished no more than the window-sash, nails, hinges, locks, and rough lumber for framing the door and window. The agency however wanted to provide each house with a cook stove, dishes, bedsteads, and also eventually a heating stove. The agency hoped the Lakotas would add stables, henhouses and gardens themselves.

---

[107] 'Pine Ridge Agency Annual Report 1882' by V.T. McGillycuddy in *Annual Report, Commissioner of Indian Affairs*, (Washington, D.C., 1882), 35-39.

The agent praised in his annual reports the 'northern Indians' who had finally come in. These Oglalas were energetic and industrious. In a moment of brutal candor, McGillycuddy reported to his superiors that "in a few years they ['northern Indians'] will be far in advance of the Indians who have lived for years on the reservations and been experimented with, and fairly spoiled by a constantly changing and theoretical Indian policy."[108] The agent's main complaint was against the long-time agency Lakotas like Red Cloud who would rather scheme than work. Perhaps the old-time agency Lakotas realized they had been settled in an area that had been condemned for farming by a white expert as early as 1869. And the Lakotas had virtually no livestock, not even very many of their beloved horses.

Oglalas at the Pine Ridge Agency had not seen Black Elk's horse dance. They did not know his power. He was just an 18-year-old warrior. This coming winter was to be the first 'lamenting' he had ever done. Before he did it he was purified in a sweat lodge, then offered the sacred pipe to the four quarters. He stripped his clothing and unbraided his hair to show the Thunder Beings he was at their mercy. He did take a robe to warm himself against the cold night, He also took his various sacred objects. He rode northwest from Manderson about four miles ascending to a high ridge that ran north and south between the Wounded Knee Creek valley to the east and the Big Grass Creek valley to the west.

At a summit he and a helper, probably medicine man Few Tails, arranged sage all around, centered the flowering branch and put offerings of kinnikinnick[109] wrapped in red bundles around it toward the four quarters. Then he began to wail to the west and plead for clarity. "O Great Spirit, accept my offerings. O make me' understand!"[110] He would lament in one direction for a while, go back to the center to rest and then move clockwise to the next direction.

He began to see the winged creatures: first, a spotted eagle in the west, next a chicken hawk in the north, then a black swallow east

---

[108] 'Pine Ridge Agency Annual Report 1883' by V.T. McGillycuddy in *Annual Report, Commissioner of Indian Affairs*, (Washington, D.C., 1883), 34.
[109] Melvin R. Gilmore, *Uses of Plants by the Indians of the Missouri River Region* (U.S. Bureau of American Ethnology 33, 1919), 55: for Lakotas the smoking material kinnikinnick was usually a mixture of tobacco and the inner bark of the dogwood.
[110] DeMallie, 227-232.

and to the south a swarm of butterflies. He was crying very hard now. The eagle spoke, "Behold them, these are your people." Black Elk could hear the butterflies whimpering. The eagle said, "These people shall be in great difficulty and you must go there." The chicken hawk said, "Behold your grandfathers shall come forth and you shall hear them."

The chicken hawk foreshadowed the Thunder Beings because a storm blew in, with the neighing of horses. Next appeared the two men Black Elk always saw. They came to earth and in a great cloud of dust were butterflies and dragonflies and the head of a dog. The butterflies and dragonflies changed into swallows. One of the two men shot the dog's head and it turned into a man's head. Then the eagle said, "It is time to perform the duties of your grandfathers." Black Elk thought that confirmed that the dog, which was a slave animal that served men, changing into a man symbolized himself. He must do what the grandfathers told him to do. But he also thought the dog was the enemy, to be killed without mercy.

The lament was by no means over. The storm worsened and Black Elk pleaded with the grandfathers to pity him but then abruptly he didn't fear death at all. He could see water rushing in the nearby streams from the rain but he did not have a drop on him. He may have fallen asleep. He saw close to his camp flames of all colors sparkling and when they disappeared it was an herb. As he looked at the herb a voice spoke, "Your people are in difficulty. Hurry. They need you."

Black Elk got up either in his dream or in reality. He looked east to see the daybreak star. It meant the wisdom and knowledge of his people. Faces unborn were smiling at him. Around the star was a milieu of people, birds, horses, buffalo, deer - all moving, calling.

Suddenly Black Elk heard, "Get up, I came after you."

It was Few Tails.

Black Elk went back to Manderson and entered the sweat lodge to smoke the sacred pipe with the medicine men. They wanted to hear his vision with no interpretation on his part. They listened, then said they didn't know if Black Elk was going to be a great man or not but he must do what his visions told him to do.

His next duty was that which most had to perform after a vision of the Thunder Beings. In the Moon when the Ponies Shed (May) he was supposed to perform the heyoka ceremony. He would do it on the grounds at the Pine Ridge Agency because that was where he would draw the most Oglalas.

Chapter 8

SEEING THE WASICHU WORLD

Only one who has seen Thunder Beings can act like a heyoka. And this role had to be done for one year. A Heyoka was a sacred fool or clown, who reveals the truth of his vision through contrary, foolish behavior. But being heyoka the vision is revealed in reverse.

That day Black Elk was the heyoka he performed in a ring, surrounded by onlookers. In the center a pot of water was boiling. There were numerous helpers and one main intercessor in the circle. Two took a dog and slipped a rope around its neck. Three times they acted as if they were going to tighten the rope, then on the fourth time they violently tightened the rope, choking it to death. Then they singed the dog and washed it before they separated the head, spine and tail in one piece. One helper took the piece, walked west one step for each of the six grandfathers and offered the dog to the Thunder Beings. The helper did this for each of the grandfathers, then turned to the pot to say, "In a sacred manner I thus boil this dog."[111] Three times he acted as if he was going to throw the dog into the boiling water, then on the fourth time he did it. Then he did it that way with the heart of the dog. All the while, in the ring thirty heyokas dressed crazily were making onlookers laugh.

In the ring mounted on sorrel ponies painted with streaks of black lightning were Black Elk and his fellow heyoka, Kills Enemy. Each heyoka had the right side of his head shaved but the left side had the normal long unbraided hair. Their bodies were red with black streaks of lightning. Each had a crooked bow with crooked arrows. In his hair Black Elk had the herb in his last vision.

The intercessor sang, "These are sacred," and twelve times chanted, "They have said."

Black Elk and Kills Enemy, mounted and facing west, sang.

> In a sacred manner they have sent voices to you.
> In a sacred manner they have sent voices to you.
> Half of the universe send their voices in a sacred manner.
> In a sacred manner they have sent voices to you.

---

[111] DeMallie, 233.

Black Elk and Kills Enemy sang this same song to the other three quarters.

Meanwhile the helpers danced and acted as if they would take the boiling dog for themselves. But finally Black Elk rode over and stabbed his arrow into the head and took it. Kills Enemy did the same thing to the heart. Then everyone tried to get at least a tiny piece of meat. They all thought it had power.

Again, a thunderstorm blew in and onlookers began to believe Black Elk had real power from the spirits. A few had seen him perform the horse dance near Fort Keogh and whispered about his power that day.

After that performance, Kills Enemy moved near Black Elk in Manderson. One of the first things they did together was to go into the hills to look for the daybreak star herb that Black Elk saw in the great vision. It was the Month of the Blooming Turnip (June) and many plants were blooming. Then they found it growing in the side of a dry gulch. It had two stems and the blossoms had all the colors of the four quarters: blue, red, yellow and white. It was easy to dig out. It had one long root and the top of it was about one inch thick.

Black Elk intended to use it as medicine.

That very evening a man named Cuts to Pieces came to him because he had heard of Black Elk's power. His four-year-old son was extremely sick. Black Elk was completely without experience other than what he had heard and seen from others. But he had to use his power from his vision. He knew something about what he needed. He had to borrow a drum, an eagle bone whistle and a wooden cup. He also needed the help of Kills Enemy and a pretty young maiden to represent a virgin. Of course he brought some daybreak herb.

Black Elk entered the tipi and sat down on the west side. The boy was on the northeast. The cup filled with water was in front of Black Elk. He filled a sacred pipe with kinnikinnick and entrusted it to the virgin. He also had his flowering stick.

He began by beating the drum to sound like the Thunder Beings. Kills Enemy blew the shrill eagle bone whistle whenever he was signaled. Black Elk cried, "My grandfather, the Great Spirit, you are the only one and to no other can anyone send voices. They have said you have made everything. The four quarters crossing each other you have made, and you have set a power where the sun goes down."[112] He went on to remind the spirits they had given him the little blue man from whom he could draw power. He explained how he wanted that power from the vision to help the weak.

He had been standing, facing west. Next he turned to the south, contrary to the Lakota way because he was heyoka.

He sang:

> In a sacred manner I have made them walk.
> A sacred nation lies low.
> In a sacred manner I have made them walk.
> A sacred two-legged, he lies low.
> In a sacred manner I have made him walk.

Black Elk's inner doubts about being able to cure the boy vanished. He wanted to cry with joy. He faced west and the little boy was smiling at him. Maybe the boy felt the power entering his body. Black Elk felt something in his chest and thought it was the little blue man of his vision. He stomped his foot four times by the boy, then put his mouth on the boy's stomach to suck the north wind through it. As he did it he was sure the little blue man was in his mouth and they had drawn something bad from the boy.

He powdered some of his daybreak herb and mixed it in hot water. This he blew over the boy, then he had the virgin help the boy drink some. Then the virgin helped the boy up and walked him through the four quarters.

Black Elk saw the boy smiling from the cup of water, a sign he was going to recover.

It was custom to wait four days before the medicine man got paid. Four days later Black Elk got his payment of one horse. Word spread of Black Elk's power and he was soon a fulltime medicine man. He still had obligations however to act out his vision. These obligations of the buffalo ceremony and the elk ceremony required great preparation. By the time he performed these ceremonies the year was over and he was no longer heyoka.

For the buffalo ceremony Black Elk had Kills Enemy help him. He needed Red Dog as well because that old medicine man had once experienced the same vision about a buffalo. In Black Elk's vision, one of the counselors while he walked the good red road south to north was a buffalo. Red Dog was enthused. The ceremony,

---

[112] This quote and the following quote from DeMallie, 237-238.

he said, would not only help the Oglalas walk the good red road but by doing that they would keep the buffalo from disappearing.[113]

Black Elk's body was painted red and he wore buffalo horns. Kills Enemy, also painted red, followed Black Elk beating a drum and carrying the sacred pipe filled with kinnikinnick.

Inside the tipi, which was a sacred place for the ceremony Red Dog had made a wallow to the east and within a ceremonial circle the red road running south to north. Red Dog had also made buffalo tracks next to the road.

Red Dog sang the buffalo song:

> Revealing this they walk
> A sacred herb, revealing it, they walk.
> Revealing this they walk.
> The sacred life of the buffalo, revealing it they walk.
> The sacred life of the buffalo, revealing it they walk.
> The sacred life of the buffalo, revealing it they walk.
> The sacred life of the buffalo, revealing it they walk.
> Revealing a sacred eagle feather. Revealing it they walk.
> The eagle and buffalo, relative-like they walk.

Flames shot from Red Dog's mouth.

They went outside the tipi where Black Elk cavorted around followed by Kills Enemy. In the onlookers were evil wizards scoffing at Black Elk, who withstood their evil power. After the ceremony people came forward to make offerings and ask to be cured.

No medicine man would admit he used tricks in his conjuring but Black Elk did that, just as Red Dog had used flammable liquid to shoot flames from his mouth. Gunpowder was useful too in conjuring. To the faithful these merely were props to enhance a sincerely believed ceremony.

The Oglalas believed in Black Elk and the fact that he put on quite a magical show only increased his reputation as a healer. And Black Elk truly believed he was carrying out his responsibility to deliver his vision to the people.

He performed the elk ceremony on a flat expanse south of the agency, hoping to draw a very large crowd. He had asked Standing Bear's uncle, Running Elk, to be his intercessor and advisor.[114]

---

[113] Description of the buffalo ceremony and quotes from DeMallie, 240-241.
[114] Description of the elk ceremony and quotes from DeMallie, 242-244.

Again, the inside of a tipi was a sacred place with the roads from north to south and from east to west.

All performers had to first purify themselves in a sweat lodge. Six men, including Black Elk and Running Elk, wore yellow elk-hide masks with eagle feathers for antlers. Their bodies were painted yellow with forearms and lower legs painted black. All had a large black sacred hoop painted on their back. Some carried flowering branches.

Four maidens were virgins with scarlet dresses and faces painted yellow. They had one feather in their braided hair. Each had a different symbol on her face: a large blue circle or a red star, a red disc or a blue crescent on her forehead. All Oglalas knew these symbols were the sacred hoop, a star, the sun and the moon. Each virgin carried either a flowering branch, the sacred the pipe with the eagle on it, the scared herb or the sacred hoop.

At this time all the performers were inside the tipi.

Running Elk sang:

> Advance to the four quarters.
> Advance to the four quarters.
> They are coming to behold you.
> Advance to the four quarters.
> Advance to the four quarters.
> They are coming to behold you.

The performers grunted like elk and sang this song:

> Singing a voice as I walk.
> Singing a voice as I walk.
> A sacred hoop I wear as I walk.
> Singing a voice as I walk.
> Singing a voice as I walk.
> A sacred hoop I wear as I walk.

The four virgins walked out of the tipi first and faced the west. Thunder Beings were always honored first. Then the six elk came out snorting and stamping their feet. One beat on a drum. The virgins offered the four relics to the west, then turned to the north. The elks danced around them, exhibiting their stamina and strength.[115] The virgins eventually turned to all the four quarters.

---

[115] Brown, *Animals of the Soul*, 17-19. Most of all and more than with any other animal the elk is a symbol for 'power over females', as well as prowess with females..

Finally the virgins returned to the inside of the tipi. Inside the ground was covered with animal tracks left by the spirits.

By 1886 Black Elk had lived for five years in Manderson near the Pine Ridge Agency. He had been a full-fledged healer for over three years. He had power. He had in all sincerity tried to present his great vision to the Oglalas. But he had to cope with a world controlled by white people too. He needed to know more about that world. Was it all evil? Were the wasichus really more powerful? Or were they like the ant, just more numerous and tirelessly active? What did the wasichus have to draw on for strength? Would Black Elk ever know?

The Oglalas talked about a show that Sitting Bull had done the year before. Apparently white people would pay money to watch Sitting Bull and maybe some other Lakotas too. Some former army scout called Buffalo Bill conducted the show. The Lakotas who went on the show toured America and even went across the 'big water' to England. Of course Lakotas like Black Elk knew something about England because they had been to Canada and heard all about how it was run by the Grandmother. America was run by different grandfathers in the east. Chiefs like Red Cloud had been there to see this grandfather. But last year Sitting Bull had crossed the big water to England and met the Grandmother.

This Buffalo Bill had to get permission from the grandfather in the east to hire Sitting Bull but he got it. Buffalo Bill gave Sitting Bull a lot of money. Rumors said Sitting Bull made one hundred and fifty dollars up front, then fifty dollars a week for sixteen weeks. Buffalo Bill also had given Sitting Bull a beautiful gray show horse and a magnificent wide-brimmed white cowboy hat. The horse and the hat were virtually all he brought back to Standing Rock with him because he had given all his money away, lamenting that the white people did not care for their poor people.[116] It seemed a wonder that they helped the Lakotas the way they did.

And Sitting Bull had nothing but good to say about Buffalo Bill. He was flashy, almost a conjurer, but Sitting Bull understood the necessity of that completely. Buffalo Bill was a man who kept his word and he fiercely looked out for the Lakotas in his show. And he did not rant lurid tales about them. The other highlight of the show called Buffalo Bill's Wild West were the sharpshooters, especially a

---

[116] Vestal, *Sitting Bull*, 251.

tiny 25-year-old woman called Annie Oakley. The sharp-featured mite was a crack shot that almost seemed sacred and Sitting Bull wanted to adopt her.

By the fall of 1886 when Buffalo Bill was recruiting Lakotas for his next tour many of the young Lakota men felt comfortable with the prospect. Black Elk was one of them. His family wanted him to stay at the agency and be a healer. This tour was going to be a lengthy one. But he wasn't married yet and Black Elk definitely had a mind of his own. He wanted to see the Wasichu world. He packed Lakota clothing including moccasins, buckskin clothes and his war bonnet. He left with about ten good friends. Buffalo Bill sent several wagons to the agency to carry the 100 or so Lakotas that included chief Red Shirt to Rushville, Nebraska.

Black Elk signed contracts with Buffalo Bill that enlisted his services for two years. He would be paid twenty-five dollars every month. Buffalo Bill would pay all expenses for travel, food, clothing, medical attention and other necessities. Soon they reached the Platte River to board the Union Pacific Railroad. They headed east and passed through Omaha and Chicago on the way to New York City. The first show in Madison Square Garden was on November 24, 1886. The last show there was February 22, 1887, a run of 13 weeks.

From there on March 31 the show sailed the Atlantic Ocean in the steamship *State of Nebraska*. Occasionally Black Elk brooded over his vision but he continued on nevertheless. He was not practicing as a pejuta wicasa at all. The immensity of the 'big water' overwhelmed him and other Lakotas. They encountered a savage storm. White people put on lifebelts but Black Elk dressed for death and sang songs to encourage those who were terrified. The storm passed but it was a very heavy sea. After one week everyone was sea sick. Some of the livestock was dying and the Lakotas were sickened even more to see a buffalo thrown into the sea and sink to unimaginable depths. The most valuable stock were their 160 horses, essential for performing. Finally on April 16 they disembarked in London, where they would put on shows for the next six months.

One of the first performances was for Prince Edward, the eldest son of the Grandmother. Prince Edward must have been there to judge the suitability of the show for Queen Victoria in her Jubilee Year. Show members must have been amused by the jawdropping royals when, as Buffalo Bill described it himself, "the Indians, yelling like fiends, galloped out from their ambuscades and swept around the enclosure like a whirlwind. The effect was instantaneous and otherwise electric. The Prince rose from his seat and leaned eagerly over the front of the box..."[117] Buffalo Bill was known for bluster but few things explode more overpowering energy than thundering horses.

Prince Edward was impressed because six days later the show gave a command performance for Queen Victoria. The Grandmother had a small contingent. They were however guarded by many soldiers. No shooting was allowed. It was scaled down but Black Elk was one of five who performed the grass dance very close to the queen. After the show she shook hands with all the performers.[118] Usually Buffalo Bill made a point of introducing notables to Oglala chief Red Shirt, who at 40 was physically very handsome and could be trusted to be tactful. This great day was no exception. The queen also 'talked' to Red Shirt.

The show closed in London the last day of October and moved to Birmingham, then to Manchester, where it would close on April 30, 1888.

In February 1888 Black Elk dictated a letter home. He had help from a person skilled in such matters and it was another kindness that Buffalo Bill provided that set him apart. The effort was facilitated by the Dakota Indian Mission of the Presbyterian and Congregational Churches. They would print such letters in the Lakota language in a monthly newspaper *Iapi Oaye* (Word Carrier) published at Santee, Nebraska. This newspaper was circulated at the agencies. Black Elk wrote:[119]

> Buffalo Bill's Wild West Show, Manchester, England
> Feb. 15, 1888
> Now I will tell about how I am doing with the wild west show. Always in my mind I hold to the law and all along I live remembering God. But the show runs day and night too, so at two o'clock we quit. But all along I live remembering God so He enables me to do it all.
> So my relatives, the Lakota people, now I know the white men's customs well. One custom is very good. Whoever be-

---

[117] William Lightfoot Visscher, *Buffalo Bill's Own Story of His Life and Deeds* (John R. Stanton, 1917), 329.

[118] DeMallie, 249-250, records Black Elk as 'quoting' a speech after the show by the queen that is preposterous. The question is: who invented this ridiculous speech? The translator then? Or John Neihardt later?

[119] DeMallie, 8-9. Translation from *Iapi Oaye* by DeMallie and Vine Deloria, Sr.

lieves in God will find good ways - that is what I mean. And many of the ways the white men follow are hard to endure. Whoever has no country will die in the wilderness. And although the country is large it is always full of white men. That which makes me happy is always land. Now I have stayed here three [two] years. And I am able to speak some of the white men's language. And a little while ago my friend gave me a translated paper and I rejoiced greatly. Thus the Lakotas will be able to translate English.

    Here the country is different; the days are all dark. It is always smoky so we never see the sun clearly. A little while ago this month, Feb. 7, 1888, a woman gave birth. This woman is called "Imim" and her father is called Little Chief. Now today they will baptize it, then February 15 at six o'clock that baby will have the law. So it is. With kindness I cause you to hear.

What he meant by 'holding the law' is somewhat confusing. Perhaps he refers to some basic Episcopalian tenets because all members of the show had been baptized and received instruction. He at least seemed to be taking it seriously. It is very notable that Black Elk admits he can speak some English. Speaking another language is one step beyond hearing that language and understanding it. He had been hearing English month after month and his memory was exceptional. He would later learn in America that tactically it is better to deny knowing how to understand English. One can learn a lot if speakers think the listener does not understand them.

On a lark Black Elk and five other Lakota men missed the steamboat sailing from Manchester to London, before sailing on to America on May 6. The six managed to be hired by another western show run by 'Mexican Joe', although he normally hired only Omahas. From London they went to Paris, then Germany. Then they performed in Italy. When the show returned to Paris, Black Elk was heartsick and homesick. He quit the show and apparently lived with a girl friend there. After that he was living with a girl friend and her family in England.

Here he had a vision of returning home. He had collapsed and lapsed into a coma over one day long and the host family thought he was dying. Then he regained consciousness. His vision told him he must get home. Luckily he heard Buffalo Bill was on another tour and had his show to Paris. This was in May 1889. He had been gone from Pine Ridge since the fall of 1886, gone for nearly three years! He rushed to Paris. Buffalo Bill welcomed him back and when Black Elk told him how homesick he was Buffalo Bill gave him money for his return travel, plus 90 dollars. This was not charity. It would appear Buffalo Bill deducted a large sum to pay for Black Elk's return. Normally the performers would be transported on Buffalo Bill's chartered ship for free.

In the fall of 1889 Black Elk reunited with his mother Leggins Down at her tipi on Wounded Knee Creek, just as he had seen in his last vision. His father however was mortally sick and died soon after Black Elk returned. Was that why spirits summoned him? The land around Wounded Knee Creek was parched from a drought. Black Elk was responsible for his mother now and he began working as a clerk in a store at Pine Ridge. His English and worldliness probably helped him get the job. The reservation had four main districts now named after the creeks that ran parallel to each other and northwest into the White River: White Clay Creek, Wounded Knee Creek, Porcupine Creek and Medicine Root Creek. About 2,000 Oglalas lived in each district.

Black Elk was fired with ambition. He was only too happy to relate his experiences abroad for the newspaper *Iapi Oaye*. And that way many Lakotas would know he was back.[120]

> From Red Cloud [Pine Ridge] Agency, my relatives the Lakota people, I am writing this letter in the language you understand. My relatives, I am Lakota. Back in about the year 1885 [1886] I stayed in New York; all along I remembered God. Across the ocean I came to what they call England. I stayed there one year, then again after crossing an ocean four days I came to what they call Germany. I stayed there one year... So thus all along, of the white man's many customs, only his faith, the white man's beliefs about God's will, and how they act according to it, I wanted to understand. I traveled to one city after another, and there were many customs around God's will. "Though I speak with the tongues of men and of angels, and have not charity, I am become as sounding brass, or a tinkling cymbal. And though I have the gift of prophecy, and understand all mysteries, and all knowledge; and though I have all faith, so that I could remove mountains, and have not charity, I am nothing. And though I bestow all

---

[120] DeMallie, 9-10. Translation *Iapi Oaye* by DeMallie and Vine Deloria, Sr.

my goods to feed the poor, and though I give my body to be burned, and have not charity, it profiteth me nothing" [I Corinthians 13].

So Lakota people, trust in God! Now all along I trust in God. I work honestly and it is good; I hope the people will do likewise...

Across the big ocean is where they killed Jesus; again I wished to see it but it was four days on the ocean and there was no railroad. If horses go there they die of thirst. Only those long-necks [camels] are able to go there. [It would require] much money for me to be able to go over there to tell about it myself.

Whether Black Elk really had such an insatiable curiosity about Christianity can not be determined. After all, the newspaper was run by Presbyterians and Congregationalists. It is unlikely at this point in his life that Black Elk could even read Lakota, let alone write it.

Black Elk returned to the agency the year of the 1889 treaty, in which General Crook and other white men of a special commission manipulated votes of Lakotas to swindle them out of half of their land.[121] Instead of having the 1868 Great Sioux Reservation of 35,000 square miles - an area as large as the five New England states combined - by the end of 1889 they had five isolated reservations of Standing Rock, Cheyenne River, Pine Ridge, Rosebud and Lower Brule that totaled 19,000 square miles. Had outspoken agent Valentine McGillycuddy been ousted in 1886 so there would be no protest from any whites? Red Cloud had been involved in that ouster and perhaps unwittingly helped the schemers that finally took half the remaining land from the Lakotas. So the mood of the Lakotas in 1889 was ugly.

---

[121] Hyde, *Sioux Chronicle* (Un. Oklahoma Press, 1937, revised 1957), 202-228.

Chapter 9

WOUNDED KNEE NIGHTMARE

The years at the agency had been flush for the Oglalas until the last 'hostiles' came in with Crazy Horse in 1877. Ever since 1878 the agency had to reduce rations again and again as the American government pretended the Lakotas needed less and less as they became farmers and ranchers. It didn't help their situation that the agent Gallagher who replaced Valentine McGillycuddy in 1886 was making a name for himself in the east by cutting rations even more. Some Lakotas were close to starving.

This was the Pine Ridge Agency that Black Elk returned to.

The Lakotas were desperate for a savior. The Sun Dance had been banned since 1883.[122] And Crazy Horse had long been dead.

Along came a Messiah. In 1889 Good Thunder, Brave Bear and Yellow Breast of the Lakotas had trekked to Nevada, a state since 1864, to see a Paiute named Wovoka. Word spread all over the reservations that a way to rid the country of white people had been revealed to Wovoka in a vision. When the three Lakotas found Wovoka he gave them sacred relics. They returned with red and white paint to be painted on the face for a round dance that was to be celebrated for five days. Wovoka called the ceremony the ghost dance.

Black Elk saw it as a chance to get back on the red road.

Wovoka's vision sounded much like his own. Was his own vision coming true? If he jumped into the ghost dance effort with all his heart would his power return and make it possible for his vision to come true? Could the Lakotas get into the sacred hoop and prosper once again? As Black Elk cogitated he wanted more and more to see this Wovoka himself. Yet he couldn't leave his new job so soon. He was actually in Pine Ridge now most of the time.

Others thought as he did all over the Lakota reservations, so it was no surprise the tribal council sent delegates from the Pine Ridge, Rosebud and Cheyenne River reservations. They went to find Wovoka in spring of 1890. Among them were Kicking Bear,

---

[122] 'Pine Ridge Agency Annual Report 1884' by V.T. McGillycuddy in *Annual Report, Commissioner of Indian Affairs*, (Washington, D.C., 1884), 37.

Short Bull, Bear Comes Out and Mash the Kettle. The Oglalas always thought it was Kicking Bear, an Oglala that ran with the Minneconjous, who murdered the agent's clerk back in 1874. Others thought he did it too. If Kicking Bear got involved in the ghost dance business and the bluecoats found out about it there would be an incendiary situation on the reservations.

Sure enough, news spread in the summer of 1890 that the Minneconjous, spurred by Kicking Bear, were celebrating the ghost dance up north on the Cheyenne River reservation. Black Elk had dithered while others rushed into action and maybe those Lakotas weren't even the right ones to understand if Wovoka was a man of truth or just a conjurer. Because Black Elk was related to Kicking Bear he probably could have easily gone with them to see Wovoka. Then he would know if this Paiute was genuine or not. But he dithered. Next he heard Wovoka was the son of the Great Spirit that had come to earth as a man. While Black Elk was signed on with Buffalo Bill he had been forced to hear preaching about this Christian religion. Black Elk was very clever and picked things up quickly. And he was suspicious about Wovoka imitating some Christian beliefs.

He was startled to hear in August 1890 that they were performing the ghost dance at Manderson on Wounded Knee Creek!

He resisted reacting to the news but then mounted his pony and careened east, then veered to the north. They were indeed performing the ghost dance at Manderson. His uncle Good Thunder had organized the dance. They were through dancing that day. But what Black Elk saw made him very excited.

'My vision!' Black Elk must have thought.

In the center of a circle was a pole. The dancers had painted their faces red. Yes, the elements of the ghost dance seemed to bear out the great vision that Black Elk had at the age of nine. The circle was his 'sacred hoop'. The pole seemed exactly like his 'sacred tree that no longer bloomed'. Even the red paint was in harmony with his vision. By carrying out certain revelations in his vision he was to cause the tree to bloom again. The blooming tree was the resurgence of the Lakota nation. But Black Elk had waited until he got older, then he got caught up in worldly things. He had pushed aside his vision. Now at age 27 he even worked in a store as a clerk. But suddenly his vision seemed to be coming to life in this ghost dance.

The next day he eagerly joined in the dancing.

Day after day the Lakotas danced.

Finally Black Elk began to have strong visions again. In one he met a man neither white nor red but with wounds in his palms. The man transformed into many colors and was haloed by bright light. Then he disappeared. Twelve men remained. Black Elk saw a green paradise with no people but strong young adults. And all red people. Then he saw great herds of buffalo. But not all the visions were so wonderful. Black Elk also saw starving Lakotas, wailing Lakotas. He became more and more confused at the meaning of what he was seeing in his ghost dance visions. Nevertheless the ghost dancing grew and grew in fervor. Lakotas were dancing on every reservation. They danced until they dropped.

In one vision he saw men wearing ghost shirts. The men told Black Elk he must carry these ghost shirts to his people. When Black Elk awoke he told his vision to other Oglalas and made an exact copy of the ghost shirt, according to his Messiah vision. Big Road and others believed the shirts had power and said everyone should wear such a ghost shirt if the nation were to prosper. He started making ghost shirts for Oglalas. He started making ghost dresses. He made ghost shirts for Brules camping at Cutmeat Creek. He even went over to the Rosebud Reservation and danced and gave the Brules six ghost shirts and six ghost dresses.

Lakotas were dancing all over the reservations.

Jesuit Father Francis Craft watched Rosebud Lakotas doing the ghost dance, later telling Father Perrig it was "alright, quite Catholic, and even edifying".[123] The ghost dance was loaded with Christian elements, which few Lakotas recognized. The savior was coming to raise the dead, restore the buffalo and rid the country of the whites. Lakotas weren't digging into where Wovoka got these ideas. They only wanted to hear the message.

But some white authorities couldn't stand for this new energy.

The dancing seemed to be reviving the Lakotas' spirits too much. So the whites tried to ban the dancing, just as they had banned sundancing and other sacred Lakota rituals. When some Lakotas who knew about such things tried to point out the elements of Christ and Resurrection in these new beliefs they were not believed by the whites. They pointed out Wovoka had told them to do only good, to never fight. Just dance and wait for the Resurrection, he said.

---

[123] Steltenkamp (1993), 73. Ironically Father Craft was mistaken for a soldier in the fighting and stabbed, seriously but not mortally wounded.

Sitting Bull up on the Standing Rock reservation was skeptical of all this ghost dancing too but he allowed the Lakotas there to dance. Because of his tolerance he became the target. He was to be 'quietly' arrested. But no such arrest could be made on a legendary chief. Soon dozens of angry Lakotas surrounded Sitting Bull and the arresting officers.

"This is not going to happen!" shouted one very angry Lakota.

Arguments began. Hands shoved. Tempers flared. A shot was fired. And as so frequently happened during such fights the first to be killed was the great chief. And that was how Sitting Bull was murdered. Within seconds of the first shot fired, a pistol held behind Sitting Bull's head sent a bullet mushrooming into his brain. So the mission for the arresting officers was a success. Dead or alive, the so-called troublemaker had been removed. The fight was blamed on the angry Lakotas who had been ghost-dancing.

Black Elk was soon to learn the death of Sitting Bull had set other things in motion.

"Chief Big Foot is leaving the Cheyenne River Reservation with his band of Minneconjous," said a friend of Black Elk. "He's bringing them here to Pine Ridge."

The Cheyenne River reservation was just south of the Standing Rock Reservation. Black Elk knew why the chief was coming south to the Pine Ridge Agency. Red Cloud was here. Red Cloud knew how to get along with bluecoats. Chief Big Foot on the Cheyenne River Reservation didn't want to be murdered like Sitting Bull. Maybe Red Cloud could protect him. Of course the bluecoats would try to stop this chief and his band from the Cheyenne River Reservation if they hadn't already. They would have to tell this chief and his Lakotas where to camp. They would have to gawk inside the blankets of this chief and his Lakotas. The bluecoats did so many things to the Lakotas one thing was sure to finally spark something off, like flint to gunpowder. That was why Black Elk couldn't sleep.

'And these bluecoats here at Pine Ridge are Custer's old yellow-stripe outfit,' he added to further blacken his thoughts.

Dawn began to brighten a cloudless sky. Maybe it wouldn't be a bad day after all. Black Elk had spent the entire night walking and thinking. He went into his tipi. He had no wife. His father had died the previous year, so Black Elk's mother Leggins Down kept up the tipi. He drank hot coffee his mother had made and gnawed on the dried winter fare of meat, turnips and berries. Then he did what every Lakota man did almost every morning of his life. He mounted his pony tied nearby and rode out to check his pony herd, small though it was. From the east came pop-pop-pop! Rifle fire. Then he heard a popping sound that rattled on and on like a crazy woodpecker. That could only be from bluecoats shooting the wagon guns. The whites called them 'machine guns' or 'Hotchkiss guns'.

'The noise from the wagon guns is coming from the east,' Black Elk realized.

This wasn't something a Lakota just dashed off to see. Black Elk cut out a buckskin - a real war pony - from his herd and returned to his tipi. There he painted his face red and donned his bullet-proof shirt that he had made only for himself. On the back of the shirt was painted a spotted eagle with outstretched wings. On the left shoulder was a star. Rainbows were around the collar and on the front from left shoulder to right hip. Of course red bolts of lightning were all over the shirt. He had attached eagle feathers at the shoulders, elbows and wrists. One eagle feather in his hair protected his head.

'I'm going over there to fight for the rights of the Lakotas' he thought, though he had doubts now about the ghost dance.

He saw how worried his mother was. He would remember that look. That was good for fighting. It kept a Lakota from being soft-hearted to the people who would hurt his mother. But as Black Elk rode the buckskin east beside about twenty other Lakota warriors he realized he hadn't brought his gun. He felt sick. But it wasn't because he didn't have his gun. He didn't want to kill over the ghost dance. But there might be other things he could do. So he continued riding east. He saw from a ridge that some yellow-stripes were capturing some Lakotas. They looked no larger than ants but Black Elk had a very good eyesight at this time.[124]

On the ridge Black Elk led the warriors in a sacred chant.[125]

> A Thunder-being nation I am I have said.
> A Thunder-being nation I am I have said.

And he chanted four times, "You shall live." Then he said, "Take courage! Think of the women and little ones. We are going to free those captives!"

As they advanced down a gully in the valley slope they found a wounded Lakota. Then they found a baby girl some Lakota had hidden. She was safe there for the time being. They would come

---

[124] Within the next decade he would seriously damage his eyes.
[125] DeMallie, 273.

back for her. They now careened into the flats. The yellow-stripes saw them. The gunfire scattered a pony herd in all directions. In the chaos Black Elk taunted the soldiers by feigning charges. He waved his sacred bow but never shot an arrow. The yellow-stripes dismounted and began firing. Bullets whizzed all around Black Elk. He felt some graze his shirt like hornets. He continued to harass the soldiers. At times he was no more than four or five lengths of a horse away from their rifles. The bullets kept missing him.

'If I had a gun I could kill a lot of them,' thought Black Elk.

The soldiers were so distracted by trying to shoot Black Elk they didn't realize that their captives were slipping away. Crouching low the captives dashed through the herd of bucking, galloping ponies and headed up a draw toward the rest of Black Elk's party. Black Elk kept feigning charges but gradually withdrew. Soon he and his warriors had the captives out of sight of the yellow-stripes.

"I want to see what happened over there," said Black Elk.

So Black Elk topped the ridge and rode down another draw into Wounded Knee Creek. The slaughter from the wagon guns was much worse than he had imagined. Surely there were over 200 Lakotas lying dead and wounded in the valley. Maybe 300. Yellow-stripes were lying about too but only one for every ten Lakotas. He didn't see Big Foot, the chief who brought these Minneconjou Lakotas here, but he was sure Big Foot was dead. He didn't know who the first shot was aimed at but he was sure the second shot went into Big Foot's head.

"That is the way with the whites."

The sun was gone now. A blanket of cloud had crept in, grayer and lower with each passing moment. Nightfall was no more than two or three hours off. The clouds would be dropping snow by then. It was going to be a very cold, very snowy night. It would be very difficult for Black Elk and other Lakotas to pick up the wounded in daylight while the yellow-stripes were still shooting at anyone with a feather on his head. And after dark it would be very hard to find the wounded. Yet the wounded Lakotas had no chance of surviving the night. Suddenly Black Elk realized that he felt no pity for these dead and dying Lakotas, even though most of them were women and children. They had gone on to that green paradise full of red people and black buffaloes. The belief was sudden but Black Elk was sure of it. He felt like he would soon join them.

'Yes, I'll probably die before this fight is over' he thought.

BLACK ELK

Later Black Elk and Red Crow sat in an abandoned tipi eating dried meat. A bullet bit the ground between them. They kept on eating. That night they found campfires of bunch of Oglalas, so destitute they had no tipis against the bitter cold night. Black Elk heard a woman singing a death song for him. It was his mother!

An enormous number of Oglalas and other Lakotas were fleeing around in the night. One camp of Lakotas coming from every direction coalesced about 15 miles north of the Pine Ridge Agency. Four thousand were said to be concentrated there.

Yet the young warriors kept milling around, wanting to fight. Black Elk was no exception. Now he had his rifle. He even threw gopher dust over himself. His war party rode toward Pine Ridge. At one point he exposed himself to bluecoat riflemen. He stretched arms out to the north and made the goose call. Bullets snicked all around him. He finally withdrew but had second thoughts and went back. The riflemen were very close. He did not appeal to the Thunder Being this time. Bullets nicked his clothing, then one like a fiery ember burned him in the hip. He began to fall.

The Oglala Protector rode up and yanked him off his horse.

Black Elk protested, "It's a good day to die."

"Nephew, the people depend on you." And Protector kept him with the grip of a bear.

Three days of care by the healer Old Hollow Horn and Black Elk was ready to ride again. The Lakotas and bluecoats were still shooting at each other on January 3. The killing had started December 29. Black Elk rode out in a war party of 60. They rode down Little Grass Creek, then cut over to the ridge on the west. Below them on White River was a detachment of bluecoats hunkering down behind their wagons, probably hauling supplies. They had been watering a bunch of horses. While Oglalas fired at the bluecoats Black Elk charged and managed to steal five of their horses. The soldiers sent a hail of bullets after him, killing two of their own horses. Black Elk was very pleased to get a white-faced bay for himself.

Then he spotted a bunch of yellow-stripes, cavalry riding hard in the creek valley. A Lakota named Red Willow was running on foot. Black Elk gave him a bluecoat's roan. Bullets were flying around them. Yet another Lakota came up on foot and Black Elk gave him a bluecoat's brown horse. A fierce fire fight broke out. Two of the Lakotas were badly wounded but escaped with the others into the badlands to the north.

Black Elk was not through. He ventured out again the next morning with three others. At Manderson they could have ambushed a cavalry patrol but the others restrained Black Elk. They were greatly outnumbered. It was certain death to attack the patrol, even to take one potshot. At Grass Creek they butchered three cattle to take meat to their stronghold. The stronghold had jumped a bluecoat scout patrol and killed the white officer. So the killing continued. The Lakotas worried about the killing being so close to their stronghold. The enemy scouts had escaped.

The next day the crier announced Black Elk would ascend a rise and appeal to the Thunder Beings. Many Lakotas went with him. Black Elk put a dab of white paint on their weapons to make them sacred. He had sacred herbs with him too.

He beseeched the grandfathers in all four quarters, then the Thunder Beings to the west. Then to everyone's astonishment, a thunderstorm arose - in the worst of winter cold. The Lakotas felt powerful, invincible. They would fight hard this day.

Back at the stronghold Young Man Afraid of His Horses came into camp. He was now accepted by the whites as the greatest chief among the Oglalas. Red Cloud was already there. After the two had talked Red Cloud said he would keep fighting if it was summer. But winter was deadly for the women and children. Bluecoat General Miles said if the Lakotas stopped fighting now there would be no further action against any of them.

Young Man Afraid of His Horses took Black Elk aside with Good Thunder, Kicking Bear and Short Bull. They were considered the instigators of the ghost dance. The whites blamed the ghost dance for all the killing. But there was no threat. The chief said what Red Cloud had said. If it had been summer he would fight the bluecoats too and make sure the bluecoats had no Lakota or Cheyenne scouts to help them. But it was winter. The women and children would suffer greatly.

Even the hotheads had to admit further fighting in the dead of winter would be very bad for the women and children. A great group of them rode into Pine ridge, passing the new Holy Rosary Mission on the way. The Blackrobes had built from their own kiln-fired bricks of clay from White Clay Creek a fine school there for Oglala children. The Blackrobes were respected. It was too bad one of the Blackrobes got accidentally stabbed in the heat of fighting. But the Blackrobes didn't just talk. They were right among the people.

On January 15, 1891, the Oglalas with Black Elk in attendance made their peace at Pine ridge Agency.

A look back at what happened reveals machinations so complex that it almost defies analysis. At least four council fires - Oglalas, Brules, Hunkpapas and Minneconjous - were involved. Every happening along the way seems fraught with 'what if'.[126] Yet the ending remains the same: a tragedy for the Minneconjous.

The general feeling among those who knew something about the Oglalas was that the intervention of the military was a colossal, murderous blunder. Valentine McGillycuddy had warned them in November 1890. In his usual sarcastic rhetoric he said, "If the Seventh Day Adventists prepare their ascension robes for the second coming of the Savior, the United States Army is not put in motion to prevent them."[127] Long before the bloodbath Charles Eastman, a physician at Fort Robinson and a mixed-blood Santee Dakota, told recently appointed agent Daniel Royer that "I still did not believe there was any widespread plot, or deliberate intention to make war upon the whites. In my own mind, I felt sure that the arrival of troops would be construed by the ghost dancers as a threat or a challenge, and would put them at once on the defensive."[128]

The new agent Royer had panicked anyway at the ghost dancing and its resulting fervor. He begged day after day for army troops. Finally President Benjamin Harrison relented. On November 19 the 9th Cavalry came to the agency from nearby Fort Robinson. That was just the beginning. Soon General John Brooke was there in command of a battalion of 9th Cavalry, eight companies of 7th Cavalry, eight companies of 2nd Infantry and one battery of the 5th Artillery. Wisely Brooke increased rations to the Lakotas. He let them chase down the beef and butcher it the old way. The army was there only to protect the agency. They were *not* to march onto the reservation. If the army had stayed put, then in spite of all the rumors about Lakota hotheads stockpiling ammunition or the

---

[126] Perhaps the best analysis is once again George Hyde. In *Sioux Chronicle*, 229-320, he devotes nearly 100 pages to the complexities that led to the tragedy.

[127] Julia B. McGillycuddy, *Blood on the Moon: Valentine Mcgillycuddy and the Sioux*, (Stanford Un. Press, 1941), 261-262.

[128] Charles A. Eastman, *From Deep Woods to Civilization* (Boston: Little, Brown & Co., 1916), 97-98.

Brules joining up with the Oglalas, likely nothing would have happened.

What precipitated the army marching onto the Pine Ridge reservation was the camp of the Minneconjou Big Foot fleeing south to join the most hostile Oglalas like Big Road on Wounded Knee Creek. To the military presence, that betrayal could not be allowed to happen. Some of the 7th Cavalry under the command of Samuel Whiteside intercepted Big Foot and escorted him to Wounded Knee. Whiteside had done it peacefully with a master's touch. The fatal mistake was made when General Brooke sent more troops of the 7th Cavalry out under the command of James Forsyth, who was to take command of all the bluecoats. Forsyth was a 'Custer-type', who "simply did not understand why he should humor Indians to avoid a fight."[129] The result was a match to kerosene: a two-minute onslaught of machine gun fire, then outright murder piecemeal of fleeing Lakota women and children just like the bluecoats had murdered Cheyenne women and children eleven years earlier .

Even then the battle had not ended with that wholesale murder but sputtered on almost two weeks. The Lakotas lost about 300 dead, including 200 women and children. The bluecoats lost thirty-one dead.

The American government quickly got rid of agent Royer as if he was the sole cause. In the annual report covering 1891 the Presbyterian missionary reported "The effect of the ghost dances in the former years was very deleterious to Christianity, and is still felt among the Ogalallas. The excitement of a false religion has left a dead, indifferent feeling about religion."[130]

Pine Ridge Agency was more glum than ever.

---

[129] Hyde, *A Sioux Chronicle*, 300.
[130] from John P. Williamson, 'Pine Ridge Agency Annual Report 1892' in *Annual Report, Commissioner of Indian Affairs*, (Washington, D.C., 1892), 459.

BLACK ELK

Chapter 10

SETTLING DOWN ON THE RESERVATION

The next permanent agent was George Brown. In the same annual report covering 1891 he pointed out candidly that no matter what enterprise the Lakotas were to undertake, that the "great discouragement to this work lies in the fact that they have no confidence in the continuity of affairs."[131] He noted a primitive practice related to issuing rations:

> The Indians were accustomed once a month to take all their children, and such belongings as they were able to take, and move into the agency to receive their rations. They always started in time so that they could visit along the road coming in and were an equal length of time getting back to their homes. The results entailed were: Neglect of field and stock and the taking of the children from the schools; also, endangering of the health and lives of those who were at all weak physically. At an issue some time in January last, during the severe winter weather, a child was frozen to death on the mother's back.

He wanted to have more points of distribution. The agent noted the Lakotas were selling their surplus stock for less than one-third its market value. He was trying to remedy that. He noted a great potential for sheep and goats on their parched land. He noted the reservation had 17 schools for 1088 children in the ages six to sixteen. They needed more schools and more teachers. He observed nearly all the older leaders and the majority of the Lakotas bitterly opposed land allotment. This was an effort to grant each Lakota a parcel of land as an entry into farming. Suspicious Lakotas thought shrewd white people would swindle private individuals out of these properties, much as they swindled Lakotas out of their livestock. The suspicions were undoubtedly correct.

---

[131] This quote and the following quote from George Brown, 'Pine Ridge Agency Annual Report 1892' in *Annual Report, Commissioner of Indian Affairs*, (Washington, D.C., 1892), 454-455.

Agent Brown, though enlightened, could not pull the Oglalas from their despair. The Lakotas were not a happy lot in the years after the Wounded Knee nightmare. Young Lakotas who had been leaning toward white ways were now sullenly bitter toward these ways. Some of the most energetic fighters during the Wounded Knee battle were ex-students of the Carlisle Indian School.[132] The Brule Plenty Horses, a Carlisle Indian School graduate, killed Lt. Edward Casey on January 7, 1891. He was later arrested but released because he was a combatant in a war. Some shrewd whites realized if they did not establish that viewpoint the 7th Cavalry had just murdered 300 non-combatants.

It seemed a time to retreat into the old ways. But the old ways had become bitter ways too. Black Elk went back to healing. He was determined to stay on the Lakota lands and help the people. He surely noticed the new presence of Blackrobes, a form of Christianity encouraged by the old schemer Red Cloud.

In 1892 at the age of 28 Black Elk married 24-year-old Katie War Bonnet. A photograph taken of Black Elk and his bride, probably about 1893, suggests he had already injured his eyes, especially his right eye. It is not known exactly how he did it but it probably involved gunpowder.[133] He was always experimenting with gunpowder as part of his conjuring tricks. He did however also use flammable liquids.

Black Elk and Katie had two sons. Never Showed Off was born in 1893, Good Voice Star in 1895. Both boys were baptized as Catholics in 1895 and also christened William and John. This timing suggests Katie had become Catholic by 1895. Black Elk did not become Catholic but being such a curious man he must have watched with interest their worship and many rituals, not to mention the elegant religious paraphernalia the priests used routinely.

Nevertheless Black Elk continued to serve people as a medicine man. He was very knowledgeable of herbs and other natural remedies. This however was not satisfactory for most patients. He had to bring forth evidence of the spirit world helping too. This conjuring supplemented his natural cures. His trademark was

---

[132] DeMallie, 280.

[133] Steltenkamp, 26-27. Daughter Lucy offered one of three stories. In addition, she was born 1907 and her name suggests a devotion to Saint Lucy. patron saint of eyes. A letter from agent J. R. Brennan in 1917 says Black Elk is practically blind.

spitting a little blue spirit into a cup of water that appeared as a fish. Nonetheless Black Elk felt very worthy actually healing people in this way.

He also could be called on to perform mainly conjuring in the 'yuwipi' ceremony, much in the way whites performed seances. Yuwipi came from the Stone Dreamers. The subjects of the yuwipi were eager to believe. Bound in the dark, the medicine man was mysteriously released by spirits. The spirits predicted future events or the fate of lost property, anything that gave their subjects comfort. It might be in healing too but that was not essential for yuwipi. The spirits revealed themselves as sounds of eagles or elk, bright flashes or other astonishing ways. Black Elk was nearly always helped in his conjuring by Kills Enemy, who was by necessity very clever himself.

Yuwipi was by no means the only ceremony Black Elk performed. Yuwipi bothered him later because of the conjuring and slight of hand. He performed another ritual stemming from the Bone Keepers. This was a very personal and secret ritual that usually resulted in Black Elk dispensing love medicine. Black Elk was well known for helping with this kind of 'healing'.

As a better known medicine man he was certainly asked to either conduct or help in the performance of the seven sacred rituals of the pipe. The sacred pipe, originally a gift to the Lakotas from the White Buffalo Calf Woman, was the centerpiece for seven sacred rites. These were real holy rituals, seeming as old as the Lakota nation itself. The seven were certainly not all of equal importance but they were nevertheless sacred. In their briefest form they were as follows, bearing in mind they often required other sacred objects:

> Keeping of the Soul (Nagi Gluhapi Na Nagi Gluxkapi): To reconcile the death of a loved one, this rite resolves things left undone, the healing of the Spirit and growth for the greater community. It allows the deceased passage into the Spirit World to reunite with Wakan Tanka.
>
> Rite of Purification (Inipi): In this sweat lodge ritual, the smoke from the pipe, the heat and steam from the fire help release guilt, burdens and evil from the one to be purified, bringing him closer to Wakan Tanka.
>
> Crying for a Vision (Hanblecheyapi): The Vision Quest makes the seeker responsible for setting and honoring limits. After a

period of fasting, the seeker prays incessantly in order to hear "the voice of the Sacred."

Sun Dance (Wiwanyag Wachipi): The ceremony requires abstaining from food and water and dancing for days. The dancers suffer, shedding their own blood so that others will not suffer. The suffering is very real and severe.

Making of Relatives (Hunkapi): By praying to Wakan Tanka, exchanging sacramental food and smoking from the sacred pipe, an enduring bond is created between people.

Preparing a Girl for Womanhood (Ishna Ta Awi Cha Lowan): This rite purifies a girl who has had her first menstrual period, preparing her for womanhood and child-bearing.

Throwing the Ball (Tapa Wanka Yap): Only girls performed this rite, throwing around a ball representing material and spiritual gifts of the universe. Not all the girls caught the ball, signifying that not everyone receives such blessings.[134]

Black Elk was often asked to help in large community performances such as he had already performed. There were many sacred dances. He had a real flair for putting on a show. It was natural enough for a Lakota anyway, but Black Elk could draw on his experience with Buffalo Bill's Wild West show and style his effects after some of that show's electrifying effects and illusions. Black Elk knew what worked and how to do it.

The white authorities disapproved of almost everything a medicine man like Black Elk did as the nineteenth century approached its end. But many authorities chose to look the other way. Denying Lakotas their ancient customs was a dangerous business. Black Elk kept very busy, either performing rituals or concocting his magic for the rituals. Compared to other Oglalas he provided very well for himself and his family. And his family may have included Katie's sister, which some have claimed.[135]

---

[134] Years later, some replace Throwing the Ball with offering the pipe to the four quarters.

[135] Black Elk DeSersa, Esther etal, *Black Elk Lives: conversations with the Black Elk family*. (Un. Nebraska Press, 2000), 151, claims Black Elk was also married to Katie War Bonnet's unnamed sister and had two children with her: Richard born in 1917 and a girl Lillian. The birth year of 1917 makes this assertion much less likely.

BLACK ELK

In 1899 Black Elk and Katie had a son, Benjamin. So with Katie he had three sons, although William had died in 1895. By 1903, perhaps as early as 1901, Katie died too. She was no more than 35 years old. Black Elk was left with two sons. In 1903 John was eight, Benjamin only four. It seems possible Black Elk's mother Mary Leggins Down was widowed a second time[136] by then and lived with him until her death in 1915.

An incident occurred, possibly in 1904, that some say caused Black Elk's final disillusion with Lakota healing. According to this story, Black Elk was tending an extremely sick boy in a tipi when Jesuit Father Joseph Lindebner came to give the boy last rites. Furiously, the priest grabbed Black Elk by the neck and threw him and his paraphernalia out of the tipi. Black Elk meekly left, according to the story, realizing he did not have the power that the priest had. Shortly after that assault the priest took crestfallen Black Elk under his wing, instructed him in Catholicism and just two weeks later on December 6, baptized Black Elk and christened him Nicholas because it was the feast day of Saint Nicholas.[137] The only certain facts about the story are that he was baptized on December 6, 1904, and he was christened Nicholas.

The rest of the story is suspect. Black Elk himself told a similar story.[138] But it happened in 1902. The framework of it however is the same. A Blackrobe angrily threw his sacred objects out and made him leave the side of a sick boy. Black Elk added with perhaps grim satisfaction that the boy recovered but this particular priest died after being thrown by a horse. That priest could only have been Father Aloysius Bosch.[139] Before succumbing at age 51 Father Bosch suffered intensely for five months from the accident. This version of the assault on Black Elk has the ring of truth for another reason. From all accounts tiny white-bearded Father Joseph Lindebner, German-born, was far too good-natured to have attacked anybody for anything. On the other hand, Father Bosch, also

---

[136] Sometime after 1889 she married Good Thunder.

[137] This is his daughter Lucy's account in Steltenkamp, (1993), 33-38. She was born two years after the conversion and admitted her father *never talked about the conversion.*

[138] DeMallie, 12.

[139] Mary Claudia Duratschek, *Crusading Along Sioux Trails* (NY: Grail Publications, 1947), 131. Duratschek is a Benedictine sister and a PhD. This book

German-born, was a great burly man who intimidated even some Lakotas.

John Lone Goose, who had known Black Elk since 1900, told yet another version.[140]

> Sam Kills Brave, he's a Catholic, lived close to him. And before Nick converted, Kills Brave would say, "Why don't you give up your yuwipi and join the Catholic church? You may think it's best, but the way I look at it, it isn't right for you to do the yuwipi. " Kills Brave kept talking to him that way, and I guess Nick got those words in his mind. He said that after Kills Brave spoke to him, he wanted to change.

Another possible cause for his conversion is that it was to honor Katie. She might have tried for a long time to persuade Black Elk to become Catholic, even explaining the tenets of that faith. Perhaps he mulled it over. Then when she became mortally ill he of course tried to save her with his own power and he could not. Perhaps as she was dying she begged Black Elk to raise the boys as Catholics.

Another possible reason for his disillusion with the Lakota religion was his failure to realize his vision. Not only could he not understand how to execute it but he would refuse to do some of it anyway. At some point Black Elk became convinced he had to use the soldier weed by the year 1900.[141] This he would not do even if he understood how to do it. The soldier weed had the power to destroy the entire white race. The thought of killing women and children was too terrible.

Whatever the cause or causes, the fact remains: Black Elk was baptized on December 6, 1904.

His future daughter Lucy had more to add.

> My father said that what he was doing before [traditional Lakota medicine]... was the work of the Great Spirit, but that he suffered a lot doing it. As a matter of fact, he had ulcers and had to be treated for them shortly after he started his missionary work. The Jesuits sent him to a hospital in Omaha, and he was on a diet for two or three months until the ulcers cleared up.[142]

---

[140] Steltenkamp (1993), 32.
[141] DeMallie, 14.
[142] Steltenkamp (1993), 35.

BLACK ELK

In 1906 Black Elk, now widely known as Nicholas Black Elk or just 'Nick,' married again. Not surprisingly Anna Brings White (or Brings White Horses) was Catholic and lived near Manderson. She was widowed with two daughters, Agatha and Mary. Daughter Lucy was born to Nick and Anna in June 1907. So for a time his household consisted of at least eight: Nick, Anna, Mary Leggins Down, sons Johnny and Ben and daughters Agatha, Mary and Lucy. They threw themselves into the activity of the St. Agnes church in Manderson.

Many Oglalas were becoming Christian, mainly Catholic and Episcopal. These two were more appealing than Presbyterianism because they were much more ritualistic and sacramental. But another form of religion that was becoming popular with Oglalas by 1905 used peyote, a hallucinogen derived from a cactus. The peyote was ingested or smoked in a pipe or as a cigarette.[143] There was also the traditional Lakota religion of the seven rites. Then there were various combinations of the traditional, peyote and Christianity.

The form of Catholicism on the reservation was in no way repugnant. The Blackrobes built fine white buildings of wood, and even buildings of locally made bricks. A yearly gathering of bands for the Sun Dance had been traditional with Lakotas. The last Sun Dance had been in the 1880s. Catholics shrewdly began their annual three-day congresses in 1891, usually held the first week of July. The congress encompassed other reservations. Attendance grew to 3,000 for the congress. But to attend the congress one had to belong to a sodality or society. The Blackrobes set up social groups very appealing to kinship-loving Lakotas. Even the Blackrobes themselves smacked of kinship. They were not called reverend or mister or whatever. Together with the lady Catholics they were called father, mother, sister and brother.

It was satisfying for a Lakota man to belong with his male friends to the sodality called St. Joseph. And the women could belong to the St. Mary society.

Belonging to the sodality of St. Joseph had requirements. The candidate had to know basic prayers and dogmas of the church. He had to celebrate Mass on Sundays and holy days. He also had to go to confession at least four times a year. He had to defer to all bishops and priests. They were sacred. Every member was expected

---

[143] Paul B. Steinmetz, *Pipe, Bible and Peyote among the Oglala Lakota* (Un. Tennessee Press, 1990) 87-89.

to have his children baptized Catholic. He was expected to educate them in Catholic schools. A member was obliged to visit the sick, help out in burying the dead, and aid widows and their children.

Then there were the 'don'ts'. He must not ever attend a Protestant service. He must not drink alcohol. He must not gamble. He must behave himself at dances. He must not give away things his family needs. And he must forego all Lakota superstitions.

Black Elk took his instruction to heart. He had a superb memory. Years later his daughter Lucy said he could even chant Mass in Latin. "You just had to say something to him once, and he caught on."[144] In no time at all the Blackrobes realized he was not only smart but respected. Soon they had talked him into becoming a catechist. The priests were stretched thin. In their absence, a catechist could hold Sunday service, lead the worshippers in prayers and hymns, recite passages from the letters of Paul and the Gospels. Black Elk seemed born to do it but he had been performing for many years now. And because he was virtually deprived of his old livelihood he needed money. The Blackrobes paid a catechist at least five dollars every month.[145]

This vocation had a future.

According to Lucy, Black Elk hit the ground running.

> [My father] was supposed to take care of the Manderson district. He gathered all his friends, called a meeting, and then asked his friends and relatives to help him build a place - a little house in which to have Mass when the father comes. Somebody donated a horse to them, a work horse, which they traded for logs. They then built the first St. Agnes Church and meetinghouse. It wasn't too big, but at least they had something ready for the priest. And so that's where my father started - right from that little log house. He was the first catechist of St. Agnes Chapel.[146]

Black Elk's mind raced to take in his new religion.

He was so thirsty for knowledge about his new spirituality that the Blackrobes would send him over the years to numerous Catholic retreats. In November 1906, after Father Buechel gave Black Elk money to go to a retreat, the priest noted in his diary," He asked 'How is it about eating during the retreat? The Indians do not eat

---

[144] Steltenkamp (1993), 68.
[145] This may have been ten dollars or more.
[146] Steltenkamp (1993), 49-50.

during their recesses.'" Black Elk always carefully compared his new religion against his older one. Often they were the same, as in this case. Fasting was observed in both traditions.[147]

After one retreat Black Elk came to Father Sialm with a solemn promise, "We Oglala catechists have resolved never to commit a mortal sin."[148] This oath had a three-fold significance. First, Black Elk seemed to have become the spokesman for the Oglala catechists. Second, the catechists were determined to live a moral life. And third, the recognition of 'mortal' sin - a sin that could result in everlasting hell - as compared to a 'venial' sin revealed a sophisticated understanding of Catholic theology. Father Sialm, who was a tough taskmaster, was humbled.

In no time Black Elk mastered the use of the so-called Catholic Ladder or the 'Two Roads Map'. He may have seen it before when he was a token Episcopalian. Protestants used it also as an instructional tool. It was an instructional tool in wide use. But for him it was for his Lakotas. It was a strip of sturdy paper about one foot wide and five feet long. At the bottom was the foundation of Catholic belief: the Trinity and creation. From there two roads ran along the strip. A golden road led to heaven. A black road led to hell. But many obstacles were along the way. All symbols were in bright colors. Lakotas loved symbols. Symbols conveyed their history. Symbols were pervasive in their everyday living.

Many Oglalas were not pleased to see this transformation in a yuwipi man like Black Elk. Years later his daughter recalled what he told her about his transformation.

> ...my father told me about the years when he first became a catechist. He said the people would scourge him with vicious words and make fun of him, since he had been a yuwipi medicine man. The people made a lot of vicious talk concerning him, but he held on and did not go back to his old ways.
>
> There's a couple or three times, he said, that people would chase them out of the house--not wanting to have them in there. They belonged to this peyote clan (at that time they were really going strong). So they chased him out and even threw their books out. That's the kind of life he led, and those

---

[147] Steltenkamp (1993), 64.
[148] Steltenkamp (1993), 80.

were some of the hardships he faced during his first years as a catechist.

> My father told me: "At first, they called me names. They called me yuwipi man and said that I was the devil. But I was a catechist, so I never paid any attention to them. Pretty soon, they quieted down and started coming to me, working with me, and associating with me. I found out that the ones who did say those bad things about me were the ones most easily converted into the church. They'd come and talk to me and tell me this problem and that problem, and by just looking at their faces I could understand what kind of people they are in their hearts."
>
> He said that "at first the little ones listened to me more than the older people. I was always willing to talk to them about God and about our Lord, who was born and died for all of us men. The little ones, the children, were really glad every time I had a service. They enjoyed it. It was the little children who were interested, who came, and listened to me. One of the greatest things God rewarded me with was the little ones. I was always loved by little ones..."[149]

Finally most Oglalas accepted Black Elk as a catechist. Even his friend Kills Enemy became a catechist. He served the Grass Creek community.

Catechists were powerful evangelists.

They brought many Lakotas into the church of the Blackrobes. They had a slight advantage on the Episcopal church conducted by the Whiterobes by being more sacramental. They had a huge advantage over the strait-laced Presbyterian short coats. In these early days of Black Elk's service there was virtually no other competition among Christians. And membership in a Christian church, urged by the authorities at every opportunity, was becoming the norm.

Black Elk was a go-getter. By December 15, 1907, his first letter appeared in the *Catholic Herald* (Sinasapa Wocekiye Taeyanpaha), a Lakota-language newspaper.

> My relatives, this year I have seen two events. Last July 14 I went to a large meeting of white men in Indianapolis, Indiana, and saw an event that nearly caused me to faint. Truly I

---

[149] Steltenkamp (1993), 89-90.

saw how they were able to trust in God; truly, because they live with God, peace dwells with them. Therefore, my relatives, show respect to the priests who live with you and obey them, and hold on to what they tell you and stand firm. Thus peace will be with you, too. Then last September 20 there was a big meeting of the Catholic Church at Bull Head and I went over there and the events that I saw were good. For this reason, my relatives, we must remember thoroughly all that the church reveals to us. In that way we will strengthen one another and good will be with us.

Black Elk was undoubtedly already traveling with Blackrobe Father Henry Westropp. The priest was young at 31, energetic and very enthusiastic. The Ohio-born priest particularly liked to advance the roles of catechists. The trip to Indianapolis was for the purpose of planning how to raise money for building churches on the reservations in general. The meeting at Bull Head on the Standing Rock Reservation of the Hunkpapas was the annual congress for Lakota societies.

Nick was doing reasonably well in Manderson. Most Oglalas lived in tipis or one-room loghouses. Nick provided his family with a three-room loghouse. They had chickens, hogs, horses and cattle, both beef and diary. Lucy remembered they "grew potatoes, corn, beans, and other vegetables. My mother helped him with this, and we seemed to have enough food, because my father built a cellar in which they kept most of it."[150]

Father Westropp was so pleased with his Lakota catechists he pleaded with the Bureau of Catholic Indian Missions to send them to reservations outside the Lakota realm.

---

[150] Steltenkamp (1993), 49.

Chapter 11

PERFECTING HIS NEW CALLING

In 1908, the Bureau of Catholic Indian Missions sent Black Elk and Joseph Cangasa (Redwillow) and their wives to the Wind River Reservation, about 350 miles to the west in Wyoming. The catechists were to evangelize Arapahoes, traditional friends of Lakotas. But living on that reservation also were Shoshones, long enemies of Lakotas. Father Westropp was naive enough to hope the catechists would stay one year, maybe more. They returned in two months.

Black Elk described the trip in the *Catholic Herald of* July 1908.

> ...we went to the Arapahoe tribe in Wyoming and preached the gospel. Joe Cangasa [Redwillow] and I held a large meeting with the people. We asked them to join the holy church of God but they did not give us any response, not knowing anything about the ways of the church...With all our might we taught them about church work and now about half of the people believe and we organized a large St. Joseph society. And they had one good meeting for them and many men and women were baptized....
>
> Now, my relatives, these people were suffering in spiritual darkness, but now they have joined the church. Therefore we should pray for them....
>
> ...our Savior came on this earth and helped all poor people. In the same manner we have one priest who has been with us two years. He is Father Westropp. He moves among the poor of us and seems to be everywhere and has enabled us to do a great deal of work....These things I want you to hear.[151]

The trip cost the Bureau of Catholic Indian Missions a grand total of seventy dollars. What Black Elk might not have told the Blackrobes was that the Arapahoes and even more so the Shoshones on the Wind River Reservation had a severe peyote problem and were nastily defensive about it.[152]

---

[151] DeMallie, 18-19.
[152] Steltenkamp (1993), 66.

It was apparent Black Elk was enthused to work with Father Westropp. The energetic priest and the Bureau of Catholic Indian Missions were pleased enough with the catechists to send them forth that November to the Winnebago Reservation in Nebraska. They returned in one month. That trip cost the Bureau of Catholic Indian Missions sixty dollars. Now the Bureau of Catholic Indian Missions was suspicious. Just how effective were these catechists? Did they just like to travel?

Black Elk was bold enough to write the Bureau of Catholic Indian Missions in January 1909 for money to return to the Winnebago Reservation. The bureau asked Father Westropp for advice. He quickly wrote back.[153]

> ...To send him [Uncle Nick] money would have been equal to committing suicide. To make him one present would plant a weed in his soul hard to weed out...His trip to Winnebago netted him a nice little sum. Don't think the harder of him for what I tell you... 80 head of cattle coming to him within a year or so.

Compared to most on the reservation Black Elk was indeed prospering. But if others needed a reminder that he was a man with family responsibilities they got it that year. His son Johnny died. On the reservation anytime a younger person died it could almost be assumed the killer was tuberculosis. It was pervasive. Black Elk carried it himself. The health of Oglalas ebbed and flowed with the vagaries of the disease. And all too often one setback was too much and the victim died.

In July 1909, Black Elk counseled in the *Catholic Herald:*

> There are many Indians in the U.S. but only a few belong to God's church; many are living unhappy lives. For this reason we should take in firmly what the priests tell us: these are God's words and so mankind should benefit from them in the name of our Savior... We are here on this earth temporarily and for he who walks the straight path and dies, there is rest waiting for him. Those who receive the blood of God's Son unworthily will die and suffer. My relatives, this is very difficult, so think of these things.

---

[153] DeMallie, 20.

In September he asked the Bureau of Catholic Indian Missions in a letter to send him to the Assiniboins in Canada. "They want to see me very much," he insisted. At the end of his letter he added in the blunt way of a Lakota, "My sister died."[154]

They declined to send him to Canada.

In 1910 Father Westropp took the restless Black Elk to the Sisseton Reservation of the Santee Dakota. No priest had lived there during the reservation period. But 1910 was not a good year. The girls Agatha and Mary, both weakened by tuberculosis, died at the same time. The Black Elk family had the wrenching experience of "two caskets in the church" at the same funeral.[155] Black Elk nevertheless preached that day, certain the two girls were with God.

Oglalas had tuberculosis (also called consumption) in their glands, in their lungs and in their bones. Research was being done by Dr. James Walker right on the Pine Ridge Reservation, which had almost the worst situation in America for tuberculosis. In 1909 Hrdlicka compared Dr. Walker's results to results from other reservations.[156] Deaths at Pine Ridge from tuberculosis were about 50 every year. The Standing Rock Hunkpapas were no better off, also losing about 50 every year. In contrast the Winnebagos, with one-fourth as large a population, had less than ten deaths every year - serious nevertheless. Physicians like Hrdlicka speculated the native populations had not yet built resistance to the disease.

Physicians admired the Lakotas themselves. Hrdlicka stated. "The people of this tribe are quite shrewd, tractable, and glad to be instructed..." Certain habits however were abhorred by physicians like Hrdlicka.

> One of the most reprehensible customs among them is the so-called 'passing of the pipe.' Whenever a number of men have gathered in a house, there is passed from mouth to mouth a lighted pipe, the mouthpiece of which is never cleaned. As there is often in such a group an individual in the earlier stages of consumption, the habit must be regarded as providing a direct mode of infection with the disease.

What was to be done? Hrdlicka urged "means must be devised for curbing the infection on the reservations and in the schools" and

---

[154] Steltenkamp (1993), 70.
[155] Steltenkamp (1993), 63.
[156] Ales Hrdlicka, *Tuberculosis among certain Indian tribes of the United States* (Smithsonian Institution, Bureau of American Ethnology Bull 42, 1909).

"suitable treatment must be given those already suffering from tuberculosis". The physicians' remedies included education about hygiene, food preparation, toilet paper and wooden floors. Oh, and kill all the flies too. Dr. Walker knew how mountainous the problem was, with a high percent of the Lakotas already carrying the disease and living in dirt-poor poverty.

In November 1911 Black Elk wrote in the *Catholic Herald*, "I am engaged in difficult work which is good onto death; let us not talk of our ways of the past..."

The work was hard.

Lucy remembered.

> Sometimes he'd be in bed and somebody would come saying there was a person dying who wanted to receive the sacraments. And so, even at night he'd go and pray for them. If they were already baptized and had been receiving the sacraments, he would call for the priest in the morning. Lots of times he would have to ride to Holy Rosary Mission [thirteen miles distant] on horseback in order to get a priest to come and administer the last rites to a sick person.[157]

That wasn't the half of it, as John Lone Goose revealed.

> ...I remember every detail of what he did because I was with him - not every day - but every time the father would come over, or when he would teach somebody who wanted to be a Catholic. I was there to help him.
>
> The priests gave him instructions in the faith, and Nick said he wanted to teach God's word to the people. So he kept on learning, learning, learning. Pretty soon, he learned what the Bible meant, and that it was good. He said: 'I want to be a catechist the rest of my life. I want it that way from here on!'
>
> So he went around as far as Norris, Kyle, Potato Creek, Porcupine, and all those districts. He'd go around preaching with Father Buechel, Father Lindebner, Father Perrig, Father Louis, Father Henry, and all those old priests. Lots of people turned to the Catholic church through Nick's work.
>
> He never talked about the old ways. All he talked about was the Bible and Christ. I was with him most of the time, and I remember what he taught. He taught the name of Christ to Indians who didn't know it. The old people, the

---

[157] Steltenkamp (1993), 55.

young people, the mixed blood, even the white man-everybody that comes to him, he teaches from the Bible, from the catechist book, from his heart.

He was a pretty good speaker, and I think Our Lord gave him wisdom when he became a Christian. For even though he was kind of blind, his mind was not blind. And when he retired and was sick, he still taught God's word to the people. He turned Christian and took up catechist work. And he was still on it until he died.

Black Elk was anything but silent and somber. Stories abound of his dry sense of humor. One example of his dry humor was naming his horses and family dogs names beginning with 'B'. The horses were Baloney, Brownie and Button. And naturally his dog was Bob. An example more in the vein of slapstick stemmed from his wild ride on the back of a motorcycle piloted ineptly by Father Grotegeers. The priest got the accelerator stuck at a high speed and, face beet-red, he couldn't figure out how to turn off the engine. They careened around for a long time, Black Elk frantically holding on. Finally the priest panicked and rammed the motorcycle into a bank of soft dirt. Both riders were launched, tumbling into the dirt. "You nearly killed me!" Black Elk blurted. But it was one of his favorite stories.[158]

And Lucy accepted it as well known to everyone that her father "was a pretty talkative man", so talkative he lost track of time. Once he stayed in a store so long that when he finally left "with his groceries, his team and buggy were gone!"[159] The horses had given up on him and clopped back home on their own.

In 1912 Black Elk had his own setback with tuberculosis. They sent him to a Catholic hospital in Hot Springs. When Black Elk corresponded he usually asked for money. The fathers knew they were obligated to pay him his salary. But giving him extra money was futile. Within a day or two he would give it all away. It was a mark of Lakota manhood to give everything to those who needed it more. In that generosity the Lakota way was virtually the same as Christ's way. It had to occur to Black Elk over and over that the Lakota way and the Christian way had many points of agreement.

Black Elk recovered. In 1913 he and Ivan Star Comes Out, another catechist, went to the Yankton Reservation. Father Westropp

---

[158] Steltenkamp (1993), 59.
[159] Steltenkamp (1993), 61.

had raised enough money to construct a Catholic church there but there was no priest. So the catechists went there and built a congregation of 130 Yankton Dakotas.

In 1914 Black Elk and Anna had a son Nicholas, Junior. Then Black Elk sent his son Ben to Carlisle Indian School. Worried, he wrote the school to make sure Ben was regularly attending Mass. In 1915 Black Elk took eight-year-old Lucy to the Holy Rosary Mission, an impressive sprawling brick structure three stories tall with its dormers. Anna had already taught her to read Lakota but the school offered even more. For the next eight years Lucy would board at the mission school most of the year and go to school. Her mother Anna did not go that day. She could not bear to think of her little girl being away so long. But Anna was back there not long after that. "Your grandma died," she said.[160] Lucy had been very close to Mary Leggins Down, dead at the age of 71.

It had been grandma who explained to Lucy why her father was praying up on a hill, so distraught. "He's crying for his brother."[161] A Lakota, like Catholics, believed the living could affect the souls of the dead. Black Elk never forgot his brother Runs in the Center. It had been grandma who one day wanted to be baptized with two of her friends by Father Lindebner and left Lucy with a fond memory. The ladies were taking too long learning the prayers necessary before the baptism. Lucy lost patience, filled her baby cup with water and went into action. The priest laughed. "Lucy has already baptized all the old ladies!"[162]

Because of her family Lucy was a sweet little girl in love with the world and all life that was in it.

> I also used to go out in the garden when I was a little girl and shake hands with the corn stalks. "Good morning," I would say to these creatures. And I would pray with them.[163]

She had a sense of humor like her father. One time she showed it with the 'Two Roads Map'. Father Lindebner came and said "Lucy, let me see what you learned about this map. " She rolled it right out and said, "Father, sit down. I'm going to teach you something."[164]

---

[160] Steltenkamp (1993), 77.
[161] Steltenkamp (1993), 17.
[162] Steltenkamp (1993), 74.
[163] Steltenkamp (1993), 75.
[164] Steltenkamp (1993), 99.

BLACK ELK

Black Elk was a great admirer of the energetic Father Westropp. The appreciation was mutual. In 1916 the priest wrote of his great admiration for Black Elk, once the 'chief of the medicine men'.[165]

> Many of the younger men who are capable are given duties as catechists, and many of them are and have been faithful companions for years, gladly abandoning wife and family for weeks at a time to help the missionary in his work. One of the most fervent of these is a quondam ghost dancer and chief of the medicine men. His name is Black Elk. Ever since his conversion he has been a fervent apostle, and he has gone around like a second St. Paul, trying to convert his tribesmen to Catholicity. He has made many converts. At any time of day or night he has proved himself ready to get up and go with the missionary.

Father Westropp continued about one encounter between Black Elk and a Protestant minister who thought he could trip up the Oglala on a theological point.

> On any occasion he can arise and deliver a flood of oratory. Though half blind, he has by some hook or crook learned how to read, and he knows his religion thoroughly. On one occasion a preacher asked him if he thought it right to honor the Blessed Virgin. The following dialogue took place. Black Elk asked him: "Are the angels good people?"
> "Yes."
> "And St. Elizabeth, is she good?"
> "Yes."
> "And the Holy Ghost?"
> "Yes."
> "Well, then, if all these honored her, why should not I?"

One more example of Black Elk's shrewd mind, in this case sharper than the mind of his overconfident inquisitor.

Father Westropp was no stick in the mud. He liked to joke with the Oglalas. They affectionately called him the 'Little Owl', not just because he wore eye glasses but because he also always had a joke or a wisecrack. He joked often with Anna and Lucy. Black Elk was crushed in 1916 to learn Father Westropp was being transferred to India. Westropp was a driving force.

---

[165] Steltenkamp (1993), 65.

BLACK ELK

The catechists' travels to other reservations ended. Perhaps, in addition to his family now missing his mother, Ben and Lucy, that was why Black Elk began to travel again for other pursuits. For Black Elk now these were not years of only catechizing. He still ventured off the reservation, although records are vague. Thanks to his nephew Fools Crow we know of such a venture in 1916. A group of 52 Oglalas rode the train into Cheyenne, Wyoming, to perform at Frontier Days. At Cheyenne were many more Lakotas. The core of the celebration was a rodeo, in which young Lakotas competed, but there were other occasions like a grand parade for all the Lakotas to perform as dancers. Fools Crow was making a name for himself as a medicine man. No one would ever give him better advice than Black Elk, who was still widely known among Lakotas as a great medicine man. Fools Crow said that on the train Black Elk took him aside.[166]

> ...He said that over the years, Grandfather would show me wondrous things, that I would receive valuable messages and signs, and that solutions to reservation and healing problems would come to me during my vision quests and rituals.
>
> Black Elk went on to say that, as I traveled to competitions and toured with Wild West shows, word of my healing and prophetic power would spread. Then people who were doubters would ask me to prove what I could do by telling my visions and performing my ceremonies for them. Black Elk also said, "Even then they won't believe you unless you perform your most powerful ceremony. One of these days doubters will come to the reservation and ask you to do it. They will do their best to discover why and how you heal. And they will want to know who helps you perform your healing and prophetic work. In fact, they will attempt to learn everything about you, but you must not tell them about your 405 Stone White Men helpers, which the Great Spirit had made available to you." Black Elk was right. This very thing has happened to me many times...
>
> ...I have always thanked Grandfather for this wise and holy man. In a way, his prediction about people wanting to know my secrets began to come true while we were still in Cheyenne.

---

[166] Thomas E. Mails, *Fools Crow*, (Doubleday, 1979), 88.

This incident related by Fools Crow suggests several things about Black Elk's life. First, independent of the church he still traveled and performed, motivated by both kinship and a need for money. Second, he was anything but a simple man; he was exceedingly shrewd about human behavior. This 'wisdom' he would willingly give to those who needed it. And lastly it suggests that he would himself never reveal all his own secrets.

The colossal war in Europe that began in 1914 bothered Black Elk. It had added dimension for him because he thought the misery of it had been forecast as generation three in his childhood vision. Besides that, he had been there back in the 1880s and he could scarcely imagine those millions upon millions fighting each other. He liked both England and Germany. Now they were killing each other. And in April 1917 America joined England's side.

In May 1917 Black Elk asked Pine Ridge Indian agent, J. R. Brennan, to write the Carlisle Indian School and request that his son come back to the reservation to help him. Brennan wrote, "The father is practically blind, and needs the son to help him in what farming he is attempting, and in the care of his stock."[167] It was true Black Elk was nearly blind. It was also true Black Elk had a lot of cattle and horses. But the real reason was that Ben had turned 18. His enlisting and fighting in Europe was beyond comprehension.

To Black Elk's relief Ben came home in July.

Black Elk's next years were busy ones within the reservation. Frequently he worked in Oglala, about 15 miles north of the Holy Rosary Mission. He and Anna often lived there for extended periods. Father Buechel built a catechist's house near the church in Oglala community in 1926, and he called Black Elk to live there and take over the work. He helped priests perform pastoral duties too, so there was always more to be done. He tried to be always available to assist the Blackrobes. Father Buechel's diary entry for December 23, 1928, reads "Mass, sermon & 12 Holy Communions at Oglala. Drove home. On the way, Black Elk & I prayed for Mrs. Charles Eagle Louse who is sick".[168] That was a Friday, a very busy Friday in a no doubt very busy week. In 1928 Black Elk turned 65.

In 1929 Father Placidus Sialm married Lucy at 22 to Leo Looks Twice at the St. Agnes Chapel in Manderson. At the time Ben was 30 and Nicholas, Jr. 15.

---

[167] DeMallie, 24
[168] Steltenkamp (1993), 57-58.

Chapter 12

EXPLOITED FOR ART

Pine Ridge Agency, neglected so long, suddenly in the late 1920s attracted the interest of whites who didn't work for the government. The first nosey white person was a young woman Helen Blish, who claimed to be interested in art and became enchanted by 415 pictographs left by Amos Bad Heart Buffalo. She was daughter of a man who worked for the Indian Bureau and lived at Pine Ridge. The young woman had lived on the agency several years herself. The artist himself was dead. Helen Blish managed to 'rent' the pictographs from Dollie Pretty Cloud, Amos Bad Heart Buffalo's sister. Of course, Blish had only an inkling of what she was looking at, so she had to solicit help from Oglala elders. Their interpretations convinced her she had a wonderful, unique history of the Oglalas from the mid-1800s to the artist's death in 1913.[169]

The next invasion was by two more young women, facilitated by their friend Helen Blish. In the summer of 1930 Eleanor Hinman and Mari Sandoz chugged into Pine Ridge in a Ford Model T. They claimed to be interested in Crazy Horse and hired the agency's official interpreter, John Colhoff. They finally melted the resistance of Crazy Horse's very old colleague He Dog and the old chief yielded much information little known to whites.[170] Then someone told He Dog the women were spies, trying to get the old chief to admit to atrocities committed against whites. This would be used in court to discredit claims the Oglalas might make to regain the Black Hills. He Dog suddenly turned to stone.

---

[169] Blish photographed all the pictographs and completed for the University of Nebraska in 1928 her master's thesis, "The Amos Bad Heart Buffalo Manuscript: A Native Pictographic Historical Record of the Oglala Dakotas". Unfortunately the general public had no access to her work until her *Pictorial History of the Oglala Sioux* was published by Un. Nebraska Press in 1967, long after her untimely death in 1941.

[170] Much of this account is from Eleanor H. Hinman, "Oglala Sources on the Life of Crazy Horse: Interviews given to Eleanor H. Hinman" in *Nebraska History* v 57 n 1 (1976), 1-52

The ladies tried to interview Black Elk. According to Hinman, Black Elk insisted they pay him two cents per word for his story, which would require a minimum of two weeks! That response the women, neither of whom had that kind of money to spare, decided was a nasty form of a refusal. The ladies heard a rumor that Black Elk was disgusted with them for interviewing He Dog about Crazy Horse. He Dog's mother was a sister of Red Cloud, who played a key role in the events leading to the murder of Crazy Horse. The two ladies could not have known whether any of these stories about Black Elk were true. They understood not one word of Lakota.

One thing was true. Eleanor Hinman was mesmerized by Black Elk.[171] Meeting him was electric. She was told the two living Oglalas who most resembled Crazy Horse physically were his relatives Coffee and Black Elk. When she saw Black Elk she was stunned. She said he had one of the most expressive faces she had ever seen on any man: "For just that fraction of a second I saw 'Tashunkeh Witco' [Crazy Horse]" Hinman perceived Black Elk carried "deeply in his heart the tragedy of his nation". Would the profound old medicine man ever open up to anyone?

Yet another exploiter arrived that summer.

John Neihardt was a tiny 49-year-old man with an enormous forehead and mop of hair on a small, no-necked face. He wrote both prose and poetry but was inclined toward the latter. His magnum opus was to be an epic cycle of five poems about the Great Plains spanning the arrival of fur traders to the Wounded Knee Massacre. He wanted to interview any old Oglalas who might have been part of the Ghost Dance movement. There were many such Oglalas still alive but the agency suggested Black Elk. Interpreter Emil Afraid of Hawk, a young man of only 24, agreed to take Neihardt to him.

Whatever Emil Afraid of Hawk said to Black Elk worked. Or perhaps it was the feeling Black Elk received from the tiny poet. The old conjurer pulled a ploy he used infrequently, pretending he had expected his visitor all along.[172] This of course was tremendously flattering to his visitor. Neihardt later gushed Black Elk was uncanny in his intuition.[173] Black Elk told him he sensed a man who

---

[171] Stauffer, 151-152.

[172] Steltenkamp (1993), 88, describes a similar incident with Father Joseph Zimmerman.

[173] Neihardt seemed amazed that Black Elk knew someone was coming. This is disingenuous because Black Elk lived on a long dead-end road that probably did not see an automobile once in five years!

really wanted to know about the spiritual world of the old Lakotas. Black Elk, as was his nature, told the man his story would require quite a lot of time. Neihardt did not flinch and hinted Black Elk would get part of the profits from the book he was going to write. To allow enough time Neihardt agreed to come back the following spring. Had Eleanor Hinman and Mari Sandoz bungled the same opportunity by imagining Black Elk had insulted them?[174]

John Neihardt returned in 1931, showing up on May 9th. This time he came with daughters Enid, 19, and Hilda, 15. They would help him record the interviews. Black Elk's son Ben was unhappy with Emil Afraid of Hawk as interpreter. Apparently Afraid of Hawk had been very suspicious of Neihardt. So Ben decided he would translate. Lucy in turn wondered if Ben was up to the job. Regardless, that was the way the interview process commenced. The translation was worked out among Black Elk, Ben and Neihardt. This agreed upon translation Neihardt would then dictate to Enid, who would record it in shorthand later to be typed by her. So the interviews would exist both in shorthand in spiral notebooks and in a manuscript of typewritten pages.

This procedure was amateurish, decades behind current scholarship. Frances Densmore had perfected the process of recording and translating Lakota vocalizations long before 1930. She began recording Native Americans with phonographic equipment in 1907 and various Lakota groups since 1910. Her equipment was portable. And yet her equipment became ever more sophisticated. She worked in the field, among the speakers and singers. Densmore interpreted the data and issued reports but best of all she would leave a priceless collection of wax cylinders, always there with the original speaker and his language, always there for reference. But Densmore was a premier scholar, Neihardt was not.

Just one of many errors committed by John Neihardt because Black Elk was too deep a subject for his level of comprehension about Lakotas was Black Elk's birth month. Black Elk told Neihardt that he was born the moon of the Popping Trees (December). Black Elk's daughter Lucy knew that December was the month Black Elk was spiritually 'born' as a Christian.[175] Her father had told her he was physically born the moon the Cherries are Ripe (July).

---

[174] It is intriguing to wonder what the outcome of Black Elk's narrative would have been with the wordsmith Mari Sandoz, who was far more knowledgeable about Lakotas than Neihardt.
[175] Steltenkamp (1993), 136.

BLACK ELK

From day one John Neihardt knew his story would end with the slaughter at Wounded Knee. That completed his 'Cycle of the West'. Black Elk, on the other hand, thought Neihardt really wanted to know about the spiritual world of the old Lakotas. Because Neihardt would craft the final product the outcome was inevitable. To Neihardt's credit he realized he was the recipient of a colossal story from a Lakota holy man. What he did not appreciate was the complex layers that Black Elk offered. Black Elk was not even remotely a simple old defeated holy man sitting around mourning for the past. That however was the Black Elk Neihardt needed for his short-sighted, limited epic of the Great Plains.

John Neihardt admitted his final product was not a translation of Black Elk's narration. His final product was a transformation of the narration into a story of a defeated Oglala who symbolized a dying culture, strangled to death by white men. In line with that was the alteration of all white influence on Black Elk. He was completely Indian, Neihardt-style. He spoke short, simple sentences that to Neihardt were 'Indian'. He called animals the 'four-leggeds', birds the 'winged' and silver 'white metal'. Neihardt hammered his speech with the adjectives 'good' and 'bad', implying the limited, shallow vocabulary of a primitive. It took skill to keep the narrative from degenerating into dumbed-down Hollywood dialogue. Whether Neihardt succeeded depends on a reader's perception. English-speaking Fools Crow, after hearing Black Elk's dialogue from Neihardt's book, said tersely, "That is not my uncle."[176]

Central to the story was Black Elk's great vision at the age of nine. Although Black Elk had come to reconcile his vision with Christianity, Neihardt saw it as totally Indian but of great importance to all mankind. The vision was good and true. It could bring all nations together in the harmony of the sacred hoop. Neihardt kept much detail of the vision but he eliminated war-like elements, the very elements that Black Elk himself had always been reluctant to implement. The soldier weed totally disappeared from Neihardt's production. Because Neihardt wanted to include Black Elk's second Thunder Being vision at the age of seventeen he minimized the Thunder Being elements in the first vision to avoid repetition. He was after all crafting a story that had to be readable. And he was trying to reduce the warlike aspect of the visions anyway.

---

[176] Thomas E. Mails, *Fools Crow: Wisdom and Power* (Tulsa: Council Oaks Books, 1991), 14-15.

Neihardt knew nothing of the Two Roads Map that Black Elk had used for years to instruct candidates for the church. If he had known of it he would certainly have wondered about the authenticity of Black Elk's vision. Just how truly Oglala was it? The Two Roads Map had images of thunder and dark beings, a daybreak star, a rainbow, flying men, trees, circled villages, a black road, a red road, friendly wings, an evil blue man living in flames, and a hellish place where people moaned and mourned.[177]

If one argued that these were archetypal images common to all Lakota visions, one would be wrong. The Minneconjou White Bull revealed his dream at the same age.[178] Yes, White Bull saw a tipi with four grandfathers. Yes, he saw the birds, and horses representing the four quarters. The horses were even the same color for each direction: black from the west, white from the north, sorrel from the east and roan or buckskin from the south. Yes, he saw a man lanced, then turned into a plant. He saw meat boiling in a pot, then lanced out by one of the riders. But he did *not* see the images mentioned above on the Two Roads Map that Black Elk also saw in his vision!

A competent scholar would have to wonder if Black Elk's memories of his childhood vision had been transformed unconsciously by his much later devotion to Christianity. Or perhaps Black Elk had consciously modified his vision to accommodate Christian beliefs but did not communicate this accommodation to Neihardt. Or perhaps he did communicate it but Neihardt dismissed it. If Neihardt had actually recorded Black Elk's Lakota on wax cylinders, later scholars could have at least probed that possibility.

A competent scholar might also have realized Black Elk could have been doing what had been done many centuries before.

> Black Elk reads back into his Lakota tradition the insights he acquired as a Catholic catechist. This is exactly what the early Christian converts from Judaism did with the Old Testament, making it a foreshadowing of Christ which reaches its fulfillment in Him. And so, Black Elk does the same, making

---

[177] Steltenkamp (1993), 95, and Steltenkamp (Un. Oklahoma Press, 2009), 117, point out this not at all amazing correlation between his childhood vision and the Two Roads Map.

[178] Stanley Vestal, *Warpath: The True Story of the Fighting Sioux Told in a Biography of Chief White Bull* (Boston: Houghton Mifflin Co., 1934), 12-15.

Lakota religious tradition an "Old Testament" foreshadowing of Christ and reaching its fulfillment in Him.[179]

A premier scholar might have thoroughly analyzed the elements in the vision.

But Neihardt was not such a scholar. He was a skilled poet with very limited knowledge about Lakotas. He was a poet determined to craft a tragedy to fit his 'Cycle of the West', his imagined epic of the American west.

Neihardt had to emphasize that Black Elk failed. He failed to use the cosmic powers bestowed on him by the grandfathers. His speech at the end of the story - much quoted from the book in the years to come - when he reflects on the Wounded Knee slaughter is a *total fabrication*.

> And so it was over.
>
> I did not know then how much was ended. When I look back now from this high hill of my old age, I can still see the butchered women and children lying heaped and scattered all along the crooked gulch as plain as when I saw them with eves still young. And I can see that something else died there in the bloody mud, and was buried in the blizzard. A people's dream died there. It was a beautiful dream.
>
> And I, to whom so great a vision was given in my youth,-- you see me now a pitiful old man who has done nothing, for the nation's hoop is broken and scattered. There is no center any longer, and the sacred tree is dead.[180]

No Lakota, growing up in a tough culture devoid of self-pity, would think such drivel. Neihardt shouts despair and hopelessness. Black Elk's whole life spoke of resilience and hope. But he would know nothing of Neihardt's story until the Blackrobes reacted to it after the book was published. And they were concerned only about the omission of his conversion and years of service as a catechist.

Did Neihardt misinterpret Black Elk's story? That he misinterpreted much of it seems likely. Try as he might, the import of much of Black Elk's narrative was lost on him. To Neihardt the flagpole incident at the Red Cloud Agency in 1874 was a prank of boys. In fact it was a highly volatile confrontation of bluecoats with the

---

[179] Steinmetz (1990), 187-188.
[180] John G. Neihardt, *Black Elk Speaks* (NY: Morrow,1932), 276.

wildest of 'Northern Indians' that easily could have resulted in the deaths of many, including all the soldiers. Neihardt was oblivious.

When the book *Black Elk Speaks* was published in 1932, it was received warmly by literary critics. They knew the man who penned it was gifted. Few thought an uneducated Indian could actually express such lofty thoughts. The book did not sell out the first very small printing. This was no great disappointment to Neihardt. He was a poet. Poets did not sell. He was well satisfied with his prose effort.

Some scholars have warned it may not be possible at all for a white scholar to convey the thought of Black Elk. The old Lakotas did not think in linear progression. Theirs was a reality apart from white culture. They thought in cycles, drawing on mythic elements, rituals and symbols.[181] Ironically, the amateur Neihardt with his contempt for western religion and love of mysticism may have indeed bridged the two realities. As far as he was willing to go. The 'life story of a Holy Man of the Oglala Sioux' as the subtitle of the book promised was a fraud. Neihardt had essentially ended the book with the slaughter at Wounded Knee. Black Elk at that moment was 27 years old! His nearly 40 years as a Catholic catechist were totally ignored. Neihardt had no interest in crafting a story about such a complicated man, especially one who had sold out to the bad white people.

Such was not the case among the Catholics at the reservation. The Blackrobes were incensed. Lucy was angry. Anna was upset. Even Ben was mildly upset. Why could Neihardt not add the story of the catechist Black Elk? Neither side understood the other. Even if Neihardt would have agreed to amend the story - totally unlikely - it was not feasible. The book was dead.

The Blackrobes did not understand the book business.

Black Elk did not understand the book business.

Whether he was coerced or not, whether the Blackrobes wrote the letter for him or Lucy did, a letter went out under his sign to Neihardt complaining about the omission of his many years as a catechist. It resulted in nothing. The book was dead. Perhaps now Neihardt was glad it was dead. He knew it was to some degree a masterpiece. Did these Oglalas and Blackrobes know nothing about literature?

---

[181] Bruce Peterson, "The Two Masks of Nicholas Black Elk" (unpublished Master's thesis Un. Texas-Pan American, 1996).

Black Elk himself was probably not that displeased. He had released his burden regarding the vision. It eased his mind. He could move on. Fate had another plan for him. In the winter of 1933 he was in a very serious accident. He was in a wagon hitched to horses when the horses bolted. He was thrown under the wheels, breaking two ribs. Broken ribs could penetrate lungs. At 70 there was some concern over his recovery. There was a rumor the Blackrobes refused to give him last rites unless he wrote yet another letter explaining his commitment to his Catholic faith, dated January 26, 1934.[182] The letter was quite a production.[183]

BLACK ELK SPEAKS AGAIN - THE FINAL SPEECH

I shake hands with my white friends. Listen! I will speak words of truth. I told about the people's ways of long age and some of this a white man put in a book but he did not tell about current ways. Therefore I will speak again, a final speech.

Now I am an old man. I called my priest to pray for me and so he gave me Extreme Unction and Holy Eucharist. Therefore I will tell you the truth. Listen, my friends!

For the last thirty wars I have lived very differently from what the white man told about me. I am a believer. The Catholic priest Short Father baptized me thirty years ago. From then on they have called me Nick Black Elk. Very many of the Indians know me. Now I have converted and live in the true faith of God the Father, the Son, and the Holy Spirit. Accordingly, I say in my own Sioux Indian language, "Our Father, who art in heaven, hallowed be thy name," as Christ taught us and instructed us to say. I say the Apostles' Creed and I believe it all.

I believe in the seven sacraments of the Catholic Church. I have now received six of these: Baptism, Confirmation, Penance, Holy Eucharist, Holy Matrimony, and Extreme Unction.

For very many years I went with several priests to fight for Christ among my people. For about twenty years I helped the priests and I was a catechist in several communities. So I

---

[182] Clyde Holler, *The Black Elk Reader* (Syracuse Un. Press, 2000), xxv, claimed that Christopher Vecsey 'made this clear' by finding documents in the Holy Rosary Mission archives.
[183] DeMallie, 59-61.

think I know more about the Catholic religion than many white men.

For eight years I participated in the retreat for catechists and from this I learned a great deal about the faith. I am able to explain my faith. From my faith I know Who I believe in so my work is not in vain.

All of my family is baptized. All my children and grandchildren belong to the Catholic Church and I am glad of that and I wish very much that they will always follow the holy road.

I know what St. Peter has to say to those men who forsake the holy commandments. My white friends should read carefully 2 Peter 2: 20-22. I send my people on the straight road that Christ's church has taught us about. While I live I will never fall from faith in Christ.

Thirty years ago I knew little about the one we call God. At that time I was a very good dancer. In England I danced before Our Grandmother, Queen Victoria. At that time I gave medicines to the sick. Perhaps I was proud, I considered myself brave and I considered myself to be a good Indian, but now I think I am better.

St. Paul also became better after his conversion. I know that the Catholic religion is good, better than the Sun dance or the Ghost dance. Long ago the Indians performed such dances only for glory. They cut themselves and caused the blood to flow. But for the sake of sin Christ was nailed on the cross to take our sins away. The Indian religion of long ago did not benefit mankind. The medicine men sought only glory and presents from their curing. Christ commanded us to be humble and He taught us to stop sin. The Indian medicine men did not stop sin. Now I despise sin. And I want to go straight in the righteous way that the Catholics teach us so my soul will reach heaven. This is the way I wish it to be. With a good heart I shake hands with all of you.

[signed]
Nick Black Elk
Lucy Looks Twice
Joseph A. Zimmerman, S. J...

The cited Bible passage reads:

> For if after they have escaped the pollutions of the world through the knowledge of the Lord and Saviour Jesus Christ, they are again entangled therein, and overcome, the latter end is worse with them than the beginning. For it had been better for them not to have known the way of righteousness, than, after they have known it, to turn from the holy commandment delivered unto them. But it is happened unto them according to the true proverb, The dog is turned to his own vomit again; and the sow that was washed to her wallowing in the mire. (2 Peter 2: 20-22 KJV)

The letter was obviously for the faithful to let them know Black Elk had not relapsed into the old religion. Of course there would be no tangible result whatever from a failed book that was out of print.

In the summer of 1934 Neihardt showed up, shameless and unbowed. With his daughters Hilda and Alice, he camped the entire summer on Ben's land beside Wounded Knee Creek. He wanted the solitude necessary to work on his poem *The Song of the Messiah.* At the end of summer he departed. His appearance agitated the Blackrobes. Yet another letter appeared, dated September 20 of that year, from Black Elk stating he had cooperated with Neihardt because he had been promised half the profits from the resulting book. Neihardt informed him there were no profits whatever. Once again, Black Elk insisted, he had requested Neihardt to amend the book with his conversion to Catholicism and with the resulting years of work as a catechist.

Chapter 13

TO THE END BUSY IN TWO WORLDS

By 1935 it seemed clear Black Elk was no longer used as a catechist. His dismissal - if that's what it was - seemed easy enough to explain for a 72-year-old man recovering from an accident. But Black Elk, ever resilient, had soon cobbled together an act for Alex Duhammel at the Sitting Bull Crystal Cave on Highway 16, just south of Rapid City. It was almost 100 miles from Manderson, so Neihardt's 'defeated old man' really got around. Black Elk had known Alex Duhammel for years and some claim Black Elk even suggested the name for the caverns.[184] Duhammel had visited him at Manderson. Black Elk also personally knew Gutzon Borglum, the sculptor of Mount Rushmore. Black Elk would be used by Borglum to publicize Mount Rushmore over the next few years. Lucy would recall her father singing on top of Lincoln's head!

Somehow, in spite of his catechist activities, Black Elk had built a reputation as a showman for these budding South Dakota tourist destinations. For a percent of profits he began doing twice-daily shows for Alex Duhammel they called the 'Sioux Indian Pageant'.[185] Black Elk's part, demonstrating Lakota rituals, was so extensive he had to camp at the Sitting Bull Crystal Cave the entire summer. Duhammel had built a circular arena with surrounding canvas-covered tipis to Black Elk's specifications. Black Elk and the performers stayed in distant canvas wall tents, notable because they were not circular. Duhammel supplied food, water and fuel.

It was not a cheesy show. Black Elk was serious about educating tourists about Lakota rituals. They performed social and religious dances. They showed how Lakotas delivered a speech, used the sign language of the plains and sent smoke signals with a blanket. They demonstrated burial on a scaffold. They demonstrated preparation of a corpse for burial, subsequent burial on a scaffold, and the peace pipe ceremony. Lucy's tiny son Georgie helped his grandfather and often drew laughs like the time he impulsively climbed the burial scaffold and went to sleep.

---

[184] Steltenkamp (2009), 151
[185] described in DeMallie, 63-66, and Steltenkamp (2009), 151-156.

Black Elk himself performed traditional religious rites with the sacred pipe, performed the burial ceremony and conducted the Sun Dance. The reenactment of the Sun Dance. seemed very real. The long thongs tied to the center pole were connected to halters on the backs of the dancers. They careened around the pole, blowing on eagle bone whistles and straining against the thongs. The thongs would at last pop free as if they had in fact torn them loose from their pierced flesh.

Black Elk even performed healing on a 'sick' boy. Black Elk had painted his own face red. He was streaked yellow lightning on the sides of his face and torso. He wore the medicine man's buffalo horn headdress. He beat a hand drum and shook a rattle as he sang a healing song. Neihardt's tired old defeated man was very busy indeed.

Was this a break from Christianity? No, but it was a rebellion against total suppression of the old rituals. If Neihardt did anything at all for Black Elk it was to make him realize he had to preserve the memory of the old sacred ways. This he did untiringly. The Blackrobes may have thought to punish him for talking to Neihardt by ending his official use as a catechist but instead they freed him to show the world the old Lakota religion in every way he could.

There is a strong possibility that at this time Black Elk had resolved the conflict between Christianity and his old religion. He was at peace with both of them and believed each was true in its way. His nephew Fools Crow told of this very thing.

> Black Elk was very interested in the teachings of the Roman Catholic Church, and spent many hours talking to the priests about it. When he and I were discussing it one day, Black Elk told me he had decided that the Sioux religious way of life was pretty much the same as that of the Christian churches, and there was no reason to change what the Sioux were doing. We could pick up some of the Christian ways and teachings, and just work them in with our own, so in the end both would be better.[186]

When Black Elk returned to the reservation now he resided northwest of Oglala. But on February 19, 1941, Anna died. For 35 years they had supported each other. Black Elk moved back to Manderson to be near Ben, Lucy and Nicholas, Jr. On Memorial

---

[186] Mails (1979), 45.

Day he spoke at a cemetery so long in the sun he collapsed later. He was after all, almost 78.

He kept very busy. No rocking chair for him.

Ex-catechist or not he visited sick people and gave advice to those who wanted it. Every Sunday he would trudge two miles to St. Agnes for Mass.[187] On the way John Lone Goose would join him and they would say the rosary together. In church if necessary, he would scold youngsters for not keeping the woodbox full. But now he needed help to rise again from the Communion rail.

If one thought life did not have much left for old Black Elk they were totally mistaken.

In 1947 he had tagged along with his family to Nebraska to earn some money by digging potatoes. That fall a young white man appeared to see Black Elk. He was shrewd enough to bring along a new red catlinite pipe. The old fox Black Elk said he had been expecting him. Joseph Epes Brown was 27 years old. He was a serious scholar, burning with curiosity about the rites of the pipe. Perhaps he was astonished to find his hero of *Black Elk Speaks* in a wall tent on a Nebraska farm. Black Elk seemed impossibly old. At times he appeared crippled. Yet his mind was sharp. He invited the young seeker to go back to Manderson with him and spend the very cold South Dakota winter. In fact, Brown was well cared for in Ben's house.

Their collaboration - Ben was again the interpreter - gave rise to Brown's book titled *The Sacred Pipe*, subtitled 'Black Elk's Account of the Seven Rites of the Oglala Sioux'. It was a very detailed description of the religious rites of the Oglalas. Black Elk was 84 that winter. Brown discovered the old man had an encyclopedic memory. He never failed to surprise people. Again, the Blackrobes at Holy Rosary Mission were agitated by their worry that people would think Black Elk had relapsed back into his old religious beliefs. Many people did think that. Few could comprehend that he had resolved the two belief systems into one. Even if they suspected it they would not admit it was possible. Brown, remarkably, also seemed oblivious to Black Elk's profound theological resolutions.

In the spring of 1948 Black Elk slipped in some mud and broke his hip.[188] In the hospital he also had a stroke. It was not the end yet but he would never walk again.

---

[187] Steltenkamp (1993), 120-122.
[188] Steltenkamp (1993), 122-124.

Lucy recalled, "There was never a day he complained about his suffering. He'd sit praying and he'd tell us, 'Never fail to miss a day without your prayers. God will take care of you and reward you for this. Say the rosary too, because that is one of the powerful prayers of Our Lord's mother.'"[189]

That was very Christian and Black Elk understood it was also very Lakota.

The stroke had caused damage to Black Elk's mouth. His teeth no longer met properly. He could not chew. To demonstrate the ways Oglalas intertwined beliefs Lucy brought a Catholic named Little Warrior into the house.[190] Little Warrior did wanagi wapiya (healing through the ghost ceremony). Ben was enthused. The most reluctant was Black Elk. Little Warrior renounced yuwipi, insisting on keeping the house bright inside. He insisted no Catholic relics should be put away. It was all about calling on the power of the good spirits.

After the healing ceremony, Black Elk's mouth was straight again. He used it to have the last word. "Next time you come to doctor me, don't let those little spirits treat me so roughly. They were really treating me harsh. I'm really tired."[191]

Little Warrior knew it was Black Elk's humorous way of thanking him.

Lucy had the temerity to ask her father about 'yuwipi'.

"That's all nonsense," he snapped. "Just like the magicians you have in the white people. It's just like that."[192]

But Black Elk must have believed in the healing power of yuwipi. He had just seen Little Warrior do his peculiar non-version of it. What Black Elk objected to were the little tricks the yuwipi men thought they had to perform while doing it. And no one had used more little tricks than Black Elk had. He had used gunpowder, used flammable liquids, hid minnows in his mouth and of course worked hand in hand with his confederate Kills Enemy. But those were days long gone by.

In 1950 he was failing fast.

Lucy cared for him at his own place because she did not have room enough for him. Finally she asked Ben if he could take him in. Ben managed to get the agency to build a small one-room house for

---

[189] Steltenkamp (1993), 123.
[190] Steltenkamp (1993), 123-125.
[191] Steltenkamp (1993), 125.
[192] Steltenkamp (1993), 26.

him next to his own. Black Elk, who had turned 87, was bedridden. Caring for him were Ben's wife and their adult children Olivia, Grace and Henry. Olivia remembered it well.[193]

> Grandpa did a lot of praying--with the rosary in Lakota and with the pipe.
>
> He got so bad; he got so weak. We took turns staying with him at night and in the daytime. He would talk sometimes, and other times he wouldn't say anything. Grandpa didn't hurt. I would ask him, "Grandpa, do you hurt any place?" He'd shake his head, no. Then he got to the point where he couldn't talk. He was always wanting a rosary in his hands. I could see that sometimes he must have been praying, because he would move.

On August 17 he died and Olivia recalled the last days.

> We knew it was coming, and my brother Henry stayed all the time in the little house with him. He stayed there at night, and one night he came to our log home and said, "I think you girls had better get over there." So my dad and all of us went over there. When we went in the little house, my brother Henry was holding Grandpa like a baby. Then Grandpa just went away. He died in Henry's arms.

Joseph Epes Brown recalled that Black Elk had told him, "You will know when I am dying, because there will be a great display of some sort in the sky."[194]

Perhaps, besides prophesying celestial splendors, Black Elk was expressing the Lakota belief that the soul of a worthy man departs the body to sail on the spirit trail, what white people know as the Milky Way. Thousands on the Pine Ridge Reservation, on a warm, still night saw a colossal display in the sky.

Father Siehr, who had known Black Elk 12 years, saw the sky that night.[195]

> I've seen a number of flashes of the northern lights here in the early days, but I never saw anything quite so intense as it was that night.

---

[193] Two quotes of Olivia Black Elk Pourier from Esther Black Elk DeSersa etal, *Black Elk Lives* (2000), 146-147.
[194] Steltenkamp (1993), 134.
[195] Steltenkamp (1993), 132-133.

When we came back from the wake, the sky was lit up, and you could see those flames going into midair. It was something like a light being played on a fountain which sprays up. It seemed like it was rising and moving. There would be some flames going at a great distance way up into the sky above us. And others would be rising and coming into various groups and then, all of a sudden, spurt off on this side and then another side and then off to the center again. It was almost like day when we returned.

Everything was constantly moving. As I said, it was something like a display on a fountain of water where you see light reflecting on the water as it's being sprayed up. That's the way the sky was illumined - something like that - but it was all in every direction. That is, it was all coming up from the east and the south, the north and the west. And they'd all converge up to the top where they'd meet--rising up into the sky, and it was a tremendous sight.

They weren't stars or meteors, but rather, well, they were beams or flashes. And there was a variation of color effect in there-the whole horizon seemed to be ablaze. That's the first time and the only time I ever saw anything like it.

Perhaps Black Elk had departed but his legacy was soon to explode like that August sky.

Chapter 14

LEGACY

John Neihardt's book *Black Elk Speaks* was resurrected and republished in 1961. This time it did not fizzle out and die. It exploded and became wildly popular. At first it was accepted as a virtual verbatim autobiography of Black Elk. Sally McCluskey in 1972, though very fond of the book as literature, was one of the first to point out forcefully that it was Neihardt speaking, not Black Elk. Raymond DeMallie went to great lengths to restore the actual transcript of Black Elk's narrative, publishing the result in 1984 as *The Sixth Grandfather*. In 1993 Michael Steltenkamp published *Black Elk, Holy Man of the Oglala*, with the shocking revelation to most that Black Elk had been a staunch Catholic for his last 45 years.

A cottage industry has grown up around the meaning of Black Elk.

The rhetoric at times is less than civil.[196] Some, like Julian Rice and possibly Raymond DeMallie, say Black Elk did not believe Christianity at all; he was faking it, possibly just to make money. Neihardt might have shared this view, although he and Rice would have loathed each other. At a pole apart is Michael Steltenkamp who thinks Black Elk totally believed Christianity; he was faking traditional Lakota religion, just to make money. Some, like Hilda Neihardt, are determined to prove that at the very last Black Elk rejected Christianity and embraced his traditional Lakota religion. Some, like Clyde Holler, say Black Elk happily believed both Christianity and his traditional Lakota religion, although he kept them separate. This is the attitude of the majority of Lakota Christians. Some like Paul Steinmetz say Black Elk synthesized the two faith systems into one compatible belief system. Steinmetz believes this is where Ben Black Elk found himself.

More often than not, the squabblers will not even agree with the preceding categories. And this is not an exhaustive list of the positions defended or of the belligerents. This book does not resolve

---

[196] Positions of various scholars are drawn mainly from Clyde Holler, *Black Elk's Religion: The Sun Dance and Lakota Catholicism* (Syracuse Un. Press, 1995), 1-38.

these arguments or a thousand others that spring from them. This book does suggest that the reader not obsess over them. Must one understand every theological nuance of Martin Luther to appreciate Luther? There is enough truth known about the shrewd, resilient Black Elk and his contemporaries to satisfy and even enrich an open-minded seeker.

For this book Fools Crow, himself a distinguished Oglala medicine man, will have the last words.[197]

> My uncle, the renowned Black Elk, has earned a place above all of the other Teton holy men. We all hold him the highest. I have never heard a bad word about him, and he never said a bad word about anyone. All he wanted to do was love and serve his fellow man. Black Elk was my father's first cousin, and so he is my blood uncle. But in the Indian custom, he was also a father to me. I stayed with him quite often, and sometimes for long periods of time. We also made a few trips together, and over the years talked about many things. I learned a great deal about *Wakan-Tanka,* prophecy and medicine from him.

But one must not think Fools Crow himself followed only the traditional pipe religion.[198]

> I go to Mass once or twice a month, and I receive Holy Communion whenever I can.

And Fools Crow asserts the univeral compass of Black Elk.

> Like myself, Black Elk prayed constantly that all peoples would live as one and would cooperate with one another. We have both loved the non-Indian races, and we do not turn our backs on them to please even those of our own people who do not agree.

For Black Elk had not only catechized Lakotas in Christianity - but for many years catechized white people in the Lakota religion.

THE END

---

[197] Mails (1979), 53.
[198] This and the following quote from Mails (1979), 45.

Printed in Great Britain
by Amazon